Spiritual Fear Factor

Living Marked by the Fear of God to
Transform a World Centered
on the Fear of Man

TIM ABRAHAM

www.xulonpress.com

Contents

Commencement:
The Beginning Introduction

"Evidently, fear is not a factor for you."
- Joe Rogan, host of the once-popular American primetime television show *Fear Factor*

"That's the whole story. Here now is my final conclusion: Fear God and obey his commands, for this is everyone's duty."
- King Solomon, Ecclesiastes 12:13

Procrastination. It's what may keep you from finishing this book.[1] Or, it's why you're reading this book in the first place.[2] Personally, I think the Internet was invented for procrastinators. Why else would digital smorgasbords of opportunities to numb our minds be one lazy log-on away? Wherever you may be, just one tap, click, or voice command beckons to an earthly eternity of mind-numbing videos, games, socializing, and the like.

As drugs are to an addict, so the Internet is to an ergasiophobic. You may have to reread that last word because you've never seen or heard it. Ergasiophobic. A person who is ergasiophobic is one who suffers from ergasiophobia—the abnormal fear of work. While most of our net-surfing habits may not find their roots in an

---

[1] Kudos for reading the first 61 words (I'm counting the chapter's title and quotations)! Only 61,382 words to go. You can do it!

[2] What are you avoiding instead? Mowing the lawn? Going to the store? The project that's due tomorrow? Good news! You still have 61,371 words to go! You're welcome.

abnormal fear of work but instead in laziness, it's interesting what we can come across while riding the digital wave.

Recently, while procrastinating, I came across a column on a major news website dedicated solely to the randomness of the Internet.[3] This week's feature? Hilarious images of patrons in a relatively famous haunted house in Niagara Falls, New York. The place isn't famous because it's a haunted house that's open year-round, although it is.[4] Instead, its digital lore rests on the photos secretly snapped of men, women, and children wandering through creepy corridors on their jaw-dropping journeys. Guided only by a trail of red lights in pitch darkness, terrified visitors twist and turn through halls, rooms, and passageways nervously clutching to one another for safety. Unbeknownst to them, they are slowly finding their way to a head-on rendezvous with a car full of ghosts careening right for them—and toward Internet amusement. As a bright light suddenly overwhelms the layers of darkness, secret cameras snap the terrified takes of this action with the fictional afterlife. To commemorate this once-in-an-afterlife-time moment, the haunted house then uploads the pictures onto a popular photo stream site to be perused by procrastinators from around the world.

After my first glorious digital stumble onto this haven for procrastination—and to enhance my procrastination abilities—I developed principles for determining my favorite pictures. When you look at a man's eyes and you see more white than any other color, you know he's scared. When a woman's mouth is opened wider than a participant's five seconds into one of those professional eating contests, you know she's scared. When a group of five people are huddled so closely together that they could fit in two seats on a regional puddle-jumping jet, you know they're scared.

We all have our own pupil-dilating, adrenaline-rushing, fight-or-flight triggers, commonly known as our fears. And, as long as

---

[3]   Breaking News Alert: What's Considered Breaking News Actually Isn't News! Now back to your regularly scheduled reading.

[4]   Bad Valentine's Day Idea: "Hey, do you want to celebrate Valentine's Day by going to the haunted house down the street?" Okay, enough of my procrastinating from actually writing the rest of the book.

we're not the ones in the line of fear's fire, we are intrigued by them. You may be afraid of heights, so you clutch handrails and never, ever look down. However, if you aren't afraid of heights, you wonder why another person is always laying low, if I may twist the phrase. Why are we wired that way? Perhaps there are deeper reasons for our fears. And, because of these underlying reasons, we aren't acutely aware of all we actually fear.

From Television to Tenth Century BC

Perhaps no recent media tapped into the public's penchant for fear more than the popular television show *Fear Factor*, which originally aired in the early to mid-2000s. The show's theme is summarized in its introduction by a foreboding voice as video of contestants eat squirming maggots, plunge into water while locked in a car, climb a metal apparatus while being suspended from a plane high in the sky, and then celebrate in victory:

> Imagine a world where your greatest fears become reality. Welcome to *Fear Factor*. Each show, contestants from around the country battle each other in extreme stunts. These stunts are designed to challenge the contestants both physically . . . and mentally. If a contestant is too afraid to complete a stunt, they're eliminated. If they fail a stunt, they're eliminated. But if they succeed, they move one step closer to the grand prize: fifty thousand dollars. Testing their fears, pushing their limits. *Fear Factor.*

They are testing fears and pushing limits, motivated by money, for all to see. The television show brings people face-to-face with their worst fears. Scared of heights? Check. Bugs? Got it. Closed spaces? No problem. Being hurt physically? Done. Eating what's thought to be inedible? Order's up.

Contestants don't face their fears alone. Fellow contestants turn into competitors before our very eyes. Their interactions reveal that each competitor neatly fits into one of two categories: "Uplifters" or "Underminers." The Uplifters see their competition as a fellow person going through the same trials and experiencing the same emotions as themselves. As a result, the Uplifters encourage their fellow competitors during stunts, doing their best to encourage them on to successful completion. They do this despite the fact that the successful completion of a stunt by a competitor actually harms their own chances of winning. On the other hand, the Underminers see their competition as nothing more than an obstacle standing in their own way of victory. Logically, then, the Underminers discourage one another in sometimes subtle and more often overt ways, planting seeds of doubt and failure in their opponents' minds.

Over the course of an hour,[5] the drama unfolds. One-by-one, fear overcomes a contestant. Someone is too scared to even begin the challenge. Thousands of dollars in motivation isn't enough to overcome what's before them. Another's mentality buckles under the pressure of a physical challenge. Some are spurred on to overcome, while some are reduced down and underperform.

Each episode of *Fear Factor* ends the same way with hospitable host, Joe Rogan, standing next to a conquering contestant. With multiple fearful stunts in the rearview mirror and nothing standing between him or her and the promised prize, the victorious contestant hears Joe say his famous concluding line:

Evidently, fear is not a factor for you.

Rogan's first word—*evidently*—packs fifty-nine minutes of made-for-television drama into nine simple letters. The single word encompasses all that's happened to that point in the show. The uplifting moments. The undermining moments. The thrills of victory. The stings of defeat (both mentally and physically!). Following *evidently* is Joe's seven-word conclusion of the contestant standing next to him. Showered upon the physically and

---

[5] Well, more like thirty-eight minutes without commercials. Most of us had to sit through them because we didn't have DVR "back in the day." I can't believe I just said "back in the day." Now I'm having a quarter-life, third-life, or mid-life crisis, depending on how long I live (or when the Lord returns).

mentally strong, that little phrase "fear is not a factor for you" affirms the worldly virtue of being intrepid, unafraid of anything, of being able to overcome fears, of not letting anything or anyone stop you, and of victory.

But, what if the television show *Fear Factor* actually symbolizes our lives? What if you and I find ourselves standing before challenges that will test us not only physically and mentally but also emotionally and spiritually? What if we undergo these challenges with Uplifters and Underminers alongside us? And, to top it off, what if you and I are not victorious in life by fear not being a factor, but instead being marked by it? What if we live in a world centered on the fear of man, but have the opportunity to transform it by living marked by the fear of God?

Almost 3,000 years before the primetime premiere of *Fear Factor*, King Solomon concludes his life-experiment by writing the following two sentences:

> That's the whole story. Here now is my final con-
> clusion: Fear God and obey his commands, for
> this is everyone's duty. (Ecclesiastes 12:13)

As Rogan's *evidently* succinctly sums up the events prior, Solomon's first sentence packs decades of his life's experiences inside four short words. Everything he shares in the first twelve chapters and twelve verses leaves nothing out. It's all there. From growing up as King David's son, being granted the most wisdom a human not named Jesus has or ever will have, reigning prosperously as Israel's king, accumulating innumerable riches, overseeing the building of the Jewish temple, to falling into sin and its shame, King Solomon looks back in all his wisdom and takes time to reflect in the book of Ecclesiastes. After pursuing the rewards of wisdom, pleasure, and work, Solomon concludes: God and his commands are explicitly central to our responsibilities and implicitly central to our joy.

Throughout our lives, we build towers of fear, often ashamedly so because of the world's values. From snakes to spiders, talking in public to talking on the phone, and experiencing emotional heights to heartbreak, each of our respective fear towers is unique. Despite the different towers' looks, they are all the same at their root. We'll come to see the infrastructure of each to be the fear of man, which is at the core of the world in which we live.

But, look at Solomon's concluding command. What are we to do in regard to God? Fear Him. *Fear Him?* Are we reading that correctly? Far from Rogan's praise of affirmation regarding the absence of fear, Solomon's admonition indeed calls for us who claim to be Christians to embrace it as our duty. And, if we do, we'll live a life far from the meaningless, worthless existence Solomon saw as he pursued all that life in this world offers "under the sun."

We find ourselves in a world that affirms fearlessness while being called spiritually to a life of fear. So, what do we do? How do we live?

The Journey Ahead

I am convinced that fear is one of the most misunderstood, misinterpreted, and misapplied concepts in the Christian faith. We can get caught up in doctrinal disagreements that ultimately don't impact the way we live each day. However, that's not the case when it comes to biblical fear. That's why a biblical understanding of fear transforms our relationships with God, ourselves, others, and the world.

Looking ahead, we'll go on a journey not unlike those walking through a haunted house or beginning on an episode of *Fear Factor*. Guided by the light of the Holy Spirit, we'll twist and turn our way from before the beginning of time as we go back to history class. Where did fear come from? What does it mean that we're fearfully made?

We'll learn about the different meanings of fear in language class. I pray God's light will then illuminate our hearts as we rightly define fear in spiritual terms. It's in this moment that we'll look at the mental, emotional, and spiritual picture of who we are and who God is. Based on this biblical picture of who God is and who we are in light of Him, we'll go to biology class and dissect spiritual grasshoppers[6] before heading to math class to derive the equation for our "Spiritual Fear Factor."

Upon such discoveries, we'll then see how we're called to live marked by an ever-increasing fear until that glorious day in Heaven when our earthly fears will pass away for all eternity. We'll experience how to apply what we've learned in our history, language, math, and biology classes to living in today's world—or, as I like to call it, the Lab of Life. Finally, in our capstone seminar, we'll dive into the details of how we'll live glorified and free from fear for all eternity. After that, it's time to graduate!

Are you up for the challenge? Don't be scared! We'll go through it together, and I promise to be an Uplifter! Let's go!

---

[6] Any book that discusses the television show *Fear Factor* has to include grasshoppers. That doesn't mean I'll eat one.

Part 1:
Learning in the Classroom

Chapter 1:
History 101: The World's First Terrorist Attack

"Terrorism has shown once again it is prepared deliberately to stop at nothing in creating human victims. An end must be put to this. As never before, it is vital to unite forces of the entire world community against terror."
- Vladimir Putin, President of Russia, 2015[1]

"I heard you walking in the garden, so I hid. I was afraid because I was naked."
- Adam, Genesis 3:10

WARNING: The following is an important message. It is not a test. I repeat: This is not a test of the emergency alert system. An important message you need to act immediately upon follows: If you are like the majority of readers who skip introductions of books, please accept this friendly, encouraging note to go back and read the introduction of this book titled "Commencement: The Beginning Introduction." This sets the stage for the entire book; you do not want to be confused. Please act accordingly. This is not a test of the emergency alert system. I repeat: This is not a test.

---

[1] No, really, he did say that.

U nfortunately, we've become all-too-familiar with terrorism. With twenty-four-hour news cycles, we become accustomed to watching and hearing about terrorist threats and attacks daily. Sadly, we sometimes watch them as they happen. Even worse, we can watch them and the associated unceasing reporting, analyzing, and prognosticating and become numb to it. In one way, it's how we cope with terrorism, as we are encouraged to continue living our lives unafraid of those who wage war with tactics primarily designed to strip away our sense of security. In another way, it's a disappointing commentary on our society when our hearts can become hardened to the tragic loss of life happening every day.

We read, hear, and say the word *terrorism* often, but I wonder if we all think of the same thing when we encounter it. Having a Bachelor of Arts degree in political science,[2] I want us to adopt the following common, four-part definition of *terrorism* for the purpose of this book. Terrorism is the:

- Violent acts or threat of violent acts
- Intended to create fear
- Perpetrated for some ideological goal
- Which deliberately targets or disregards the safety of non-combatants (e.g., non-military personnel or civilians)

An Eyewitness Account

Keep this definition in mind as we go back to the account of the first terrorist attack committed in history. In Genesis 2:25, we have a detailed on-the-ground (and in-the-skies) eyewitness account of the attack provided by the Holy Spirit through Moses' inspired written record. The synopsis of the attack concludes at the end of Genesis 3.

Let's review the historical account with added snippets of my commentary as we begin our first history lesson in Genesis 2:25:

---

[2] For a political science major, I'm not a big fan of politics. I do pray and vote, though!

> Now the man and his wife [Adam and Eve] were
> both naked, but they felt no shame.

Birds are chirping as they fly across a perfect blue sky and then come to rest on branches of trees lusciously full of fruit and leaves. The bright sun highlights the movement of calmly flowing, crystal clear water that sounds like a full symphony supporting the birds singing their solos to glorify God. The shade under the trees refreshes animal and human alike. Adam works with pleasure with Eve—God's special gift to him as his mate—who is a supporting and helpful companion.

Life is perfect in the Garden of Eden. No shame. No fear. Adam and Eve are not directly involved in any physical or spiritual war right now. It's paradise.

> The serpent was the shrewdest of all the wild ani-
> mals the LORD God had made. One day he asked
> the woman, "Did God really say you must not
> eat the fruit from any of the trees in the garden?"
> (Genesis 3:1)

He is a shrewd serpent—a sly snake. With evil ideological motives unknown to Adam and Eve, the Devil enters the tranquility with terror on his mind. It's almost as if the first layers of paradise are slowly beginning to fall away.

> "Of course we may eat fruit from the trees in the
> garden," the woman replied. [3] "It's only the fruit
> from the tree in the middle of the garden that we
> are not allowed to eat. God said, 'You must not
> eat it or even touch it; if you do, you will die.'"
> (Genesis 3:2–3)

Have you ever played "the telephone game?" You know, the one where the first person of a group tells the next person a message, and then one-by-one each person must then pass the message on. Invariably, the message quoted by the very last person to receive it differs drastically from the original. Whoever thought of this game or experiment could have based it off this biblical exchange. Somehow, Eve doesn't say the original command God gives, wrongly adding that touching the tree will cause death. Did Adam tell her correctly? Did Eve misunderstand it? Regardless, it's wrong.

> "You won't die!" the serpent replied to the woman.
> [5] "God knows that your eyes will be opened as soon as you eat it, and you will be like God, knowing both good and evil." (Genesis 3:4–5)

Satan launches his attack, fully aware of and disregarding the dire eternal consequences awaiting Eve and, eventually, Adam. His weapon of choice is a pure, bold-faced lie appealing to Eve's curiosity and pride. The thoughts in Eve's mind are racing, wondering if God is holding back something better from her. Appealing to her sense of sight, sense of taste, and desire for greater wisdom, the thoughts race faster and roar louder, muffling the God-glorifying sounds of paradise.

> The woman was convinced. She saw that the tree was beautiful and its fruit looked delicious, and she wanted the wisdom it would give her. So she took some of the fruit and ate it. Then she gave some to her husband, who was with her, and he ate it, too. [7] At that moment their eyes were opened, and they suddenly felt shame at their nakedness. So they sewed fig leaves together to cover themselves. (Genesis 3:6–7)

The treacherous attack is over. Eve likely convinces Adam in the same manner, resulting in him disobeying God's command to not eat of the tree's fruit. At this moment, Adam and Eve suffer as victims, and Satan accomplishes his goal. Sin, shame, and fear are born.

> When the cool evening breezes were blowing, the
> man and his wife heard the LORD God walking
> about in the garden. So they hid from the LORD
> God among the trees. [9] Then the LORD God called
> to the man, "Where are you?"
>
> [10] He replied, "I heard you walking in the garden,
> so I hid. I was afraid because I was naked."
> (Genesis 3:8–10)

Like shrapnel from an explosion, fear and shame are lodged in
Adam and Eve's hearts, therefore destroying full, complete, intimate, and perfect fellowship with God.

> "Who told you that you were naked?" the LORD
> God asked. "Have you eaten from the tree whose
> fruit I commanded you not to eat?"
>
> [12] The man replied, "It was the woman you gave
> me who gave me the fruit, and I ate it."
>
> [13] Then the LORD God asked the woman, "What
> have you done?"
>
> "The serpent deceived me," she replied. "That's
> why I ate it." (Genesis 3:11–13)

As if God doesn't know, Adam and Eve are playing the classic
"blame game," passing the buck and responsibility.

> Then the LORD God said to the serpent, "Because
> you have done this, you are cursed more than all
> animals, domestic and wild. You will crawl on
> your belly, groveling in the dust as long as you
> live. [15] And I will cause hostility between you and
> the woman, and between your offspring and her

offspring. He will strike your head, and you will
strike his heel." (Genesis 3:14–15)

God foretells His strategy of salvation for winning the war.
While Satan may think he wins the battle, God already declares
His victory of the war.

Then he said to the woman, "I will sharpen the
pain of your pregnancy, and in pain you will give
birth. And you will desire to control your husband,
but he will rule over you."

[17] And to the man he said, "Since you listened
to your wife and ate from the tree whose fruit I
commanded you not to eat, the ground is cursed
because of you. All your life you will struggle to
scratch a living from it. [18] It will grow thorns and
thistles for you, though you will eat of its grains. [19]
By the sweat of your brow will you have food to
eat until you return to the ground from which you
were made. For you were made from dust, and to
dust you will return."

[20] Then the man—Adam—named his wife Eve,
because she would be the mother of all who live.
[21] And the LORD God made clothing from animal
skins for Adam and his wife.

[22] Then the LORD God said, "Look, the human
beings have become like us, knowing both good
and evil. What if they reach out, take fruit from
the tree of life, and eat it? Then they will live forever!" [23] So the LORD God banished them from the
Garden of Eden, and he sent Adam out to cultivate
the ground from which he had been made. [24] After
sending them out, the LORD God stationed mighty
cherubim to the east of the Garden of Eden. And

he placed a flaming sword that flashed back and
forth to guard the way to the tree of life. (Genesis
3:16–24)

In the rubble of a bomb of eternal proportion, we comb through
and search the debris to find increased labor pains, marital problems, a cursed earth, laborious lives, and ultimately death. In short,
all we recover at the scene of the attack is paradise lost.

Do you see how this is the world's first terrorist attack? We'll
look deeper into the attack with our common components of terrorism in mind:

- Violent acts or threat of violent acts
- Intended to create fear
- Perpetrated for some ideological goal
- Which deliberately targets or disregards the safety of
  non-combatants (e.g., non-military personnel or civilians)

Life before the Attack

To fully understand the magnitude of this first terrorist attack, we
can't miss all that Genesis 2:25 tells us. In the beginning, Adam and
Eve enjoy a perfect, loving relationship with God and each other—
without fear. The fact that Adam and Eve are naked means much
more than the physical fact they aren't wearing any clothes. Think
about the history of the world to this point. God creates the heavens
and earth and everything that inhabits them—including humans—
and sees that all is good. To be considered "good" to a holy and
perfect God means everything created is in its original, perfect state.

Adam and Eve relate to God in such an intimate way that they
are completely bare—physically, mentally, emotionally, and spiritually—before Him. They have nothing to hide. They walk and
talk with Him. They stand before a perfect, holy God without fear.
Without fear. That's a hard concept for us to grasp. I like to try and
think of it this way: Have you ever tried staring at the sun?[3] The

---

[3] Speaking from (an inexplicable and inexcusable) personal experience, I don't
recommend it. Ouch!

25

sun is so bright that we physically can't look directly at it for even a couple seconds without protective lenses. Further, we know that God is light, brighter than the sun. Imagine being able to literally walk intimately and full of pleasure with someone brighter than the sun. That's what Adam and Eve enjoy in paradise.

But that enjoyment and life as they know it changes dramatically because of Satan, the mastermind terrorist who plans and successfully carries out the terrorist attack.

Orchestrating the Attack

We often think of Osama bin Laden and other radicalized extremists as the masterminds of terrorist attacks. The first 6 verses of Genesis chapter 3 recount the evil one who plots and orchestrates the original terrorist attack against humanity: Satan himself.

Let's quickly go through the facts of the attack:

Satan furthers his rebellious agenda against God. This is seen in the first part of verse 1 in chapter 3. Satan, in the form of a serpent, is described as cunning, crafty, and shrewd. The original language paints a word picture for what Satan is—all with negative connotations. Jesus tells us in Luke 10:18 that He saw Satan fall from Heaven. While it's the subject of another book altogether, we can gather from Scriptures that Satan becomes prideful and wants to become like God. For example, Satan tempts Jesus for a third time in the wilderness by offering all the kingdoms of the world and their glory if only Jesus will worship him.[4] Satan wants to be God, yet all He has to offer is what God allows him to have in the first place. David writes in Psalm 24:1, "The earth is the LORD's, and everything in it. The world and all its people belong to him." Similarly, Jesus tells His disciples, "I have been given all authority in heaven and on earth." When Satan tempts Jesus, his best offer is one that, in eternity, he cannot even provide.

---

[4] Matthew 4:8–9 (ESV): Again, the devil took him [Jesus] to a very high mountain and showed him all the kingdoms of the world and their glory. ⁹ And he said to him, "All these I will give you, if you will fall down and worship me."

After God casts him down at some point prior to this attack in the Garden of Eden, Satan continues his rebellion toward God—bringing God's creation into it, as well. Make no mistake, Satan's attack is not directed toward Adam and Eve, but to God Himself. Look how Satan carries out his attack in the second half of verse 1 through verse 5: Satan manipulates and deceives Eve by intentionally distorting the truth. Satan plants the seed with the question: "Did God really say you must not eat the fruit from any of the trees in the garden?" Then, Satan capitalizes on Eve's distortion of God's direction given previously, which was the following:

> But the LORD God warned him, "You may freely eat the fruit of every tree in the garden— [17] except the tree of the knowledge of good and evil. If you eat its fruit, you are sure to die." (Genesis 2:16–17)

Perhaps this is the first time a married couple doesn't communicate well. We don't know. All we know is that the message God gives Adam—which we can logically assume Adam communicated to Eve—did not match what Eve tells the serpent.

Nowhere does God say the tree can't be touched, as Eve says. After capitalizing on her misunderstanding of God's spoken word, Satan tempts Eve with *exactly* the same desire that got him kicked down out of Heaven: The idea of being like God. Satan baits Eve with the same bait he took at some prior point in eternity past.

We know the rest of the facts: Eve eats the fruit, directly violating God's direction, then gives some to Adam, and leads him to do the same. It's in this moment in verse 6 that Satan's attack destroys human life as it was previously known, victimizing all of humanity with a life of sin and death. A terrorist deliberately targets or disregards the safety of non-combatants. In this sense, Adam and Eve—and you, I, and all of humanity—are the victims of Satan's terrorist attack in his rebellion against God. The goal of a terrorist attack is to create fear, and that's exactly what Satan does at a magnitude infinitely greater than any terrorist attack since.

All of humanity is full of fear.

Fear and the Fall

As we see, one result of Satan's attack—"the Fall" as it's commonly known—is fear. Look at the historical narrative:

> At that moment their eyes were opened, and they suddenly felt shame at their nakedness. So they sewed fig leaves together to cover themselves.
>
> [8] When the cool evening breezes were blowing, the man and his wife heard the LORD God walking about in the garden. So they hid from the LORD God among the trees. [9] Then the LORD God called to the man, "Where are you?"
>
> [10] He replied, "I heard you walking in the garden, so I hid. I was afraid because I was naked."
>
> [11] "Who told you that you were naked?" the LORD God asked. "Have you eaten from the tree whose fruit I commanded you not to eat?"
>
> [12] The man replied, "It was the woman you gave me who gave me the fruit, and I ate it."
>
> [13] Then the LORD God asked the woman, "What have you done?"
>
> "The serpent deceived me," she replied. "That's why I ate it." (Genesis 3:7–13)

In these seven verses, we see three ways Adam and Eve—and ultimately you and I—experience fear. We experience fear regarding *ourselves, others,* and *God.*

In the first half of verse 7, we see that Adam and Eve's eyes are opened. This doesn't mean they had been walking around with their eyes closed or suffered blindness before; it means that something changes in their innermost being—in their hearts. Suddenly, they both know good and evil. They both recognize that they directly violated God's command when they ate the forbidden fruit. They recognize their actions are evil. Fear grips their inner being. Continuing today, we experience fear regarding ourselves in our hearts and minds. The first effect of the Fall is fear regarding ourselves.

The second half of verse 7 illustrates that we experience fear regarding others. Suddenly, Adam is not just thinking about his own nakedness and shame. Likewise, Eve is not just thinking to herself about her own shame and nakedness. Now, they see the same in each other. Adam sees that what Eve did was wrong and that she is physically naked, just as Eve sees the same when looking at Adam. Both gripped with a new-found, never-before-experienced fear, they try to assuage this new knowledge and emotion by hastily sewing together clothes made of fig leaves.

Third and ultimately, we experience fear regarding God, as seen in verses 8–13.

Notice Adam's response to God's rhetorical question in verse 10, paraphrased: "I heard you, I was afraid, and I hid." Adam was *afraid* of God.

Adam and Eve go from a perfect, intimate relationship, walking with God, to hiding from Him—even though God knows exactly where they are and what they've done. Adam and Eve are like little children hiding in plain sight of their Father, who knows fully well what they did.

Continuing to act like little children, Adam and Eve engage in the first recorded marriage fight as Adam blames Eve and Eve then blames the serpent.[5]

Does any of this sound familiar? It should—because it's us.

The First Responder to the Attack

In the crisis management and emergency response fields, the term "tabletop exercise" is well-known and often-practiced. During

---

[5] Aren't you glad your marital (or non-marital) spats aren't recorded in a book for all to see for thousands of years?

such exercises, various teams meet to discuss how they will work in response to a crisis or emergency scenario. As different teams begin to talk about their plans, issues often arise regarding communication and coordination across the multiple teams involved in the response. This discussion occurs in a venue similar to a common business meeting around a conference room table, hence the name "tabletop exercise." The goal of tabletop exercises is to develop plans with the goal of foreseeing and mitigating as many issues that may arise that would prevent an optimal response. The exercise helps prepare first responders before an emergency or crisis actually occurs.

With God, no tabletop exercises are needed for His perfect crisis response plan prepared in eternity past. In Genesis 2:14–24, we see God allude to His plan to save and restore humanity in the aftermath of the world's first terrorist attack. Look at how, in the short-term, God cares for Adam and Eve's immediate needs. He improves and upgrades their clothes, going high class by changing their wardrobe from fig leaves to a new and improved line of animal skins.[6] Like then, He cares for our immediate needs today.

Finally, in the long-term, God cares for all of humanity by sending the Ultimate First Responder, Jesus Christ, to the scene of the world's most historic and devastating terrorist attack. Alluded to in Genesis 3:15 and then described in John 3:16, God tells Satan that ultimately Jesus will prevail when He comes to earth, lives a sinless life, dies sacrificially, and conquers death by rising after three days. And why? So that Adam, Eve, you, and I will no longer be victims of Satan's terrorist attack but will instead live forever in perfect intimacy with God as Adam and Eve once did.

Current terrorist attacks can grip us today and tomorrow, but the world's first terrorist attack can grip us for all eternity. It's only fitting, then, to listen to the words of Jesus—the Ultimate First Responder—as recorded in the beginning of Matthew 17:

---

[6] I can see it now: And here comes Eve walking in this year's hottest fashion fur. Check out Adam as he's sporting a new line of work clothes that are both durable and breathable. Prehistoric social media is blowing up!

Six days later Jesus took Peter and the two brothers, James and John, and led them up a high mountain to be alone. [2] As the men watched, Jesus' appearance was transformed so that his face shone like the sun, and his clothes became as white as light. [3] Suddenly, Moses and Elijah appeared and began talking with Jesus.

[4] Peter exclaimed, "Lord, it's wonderful for us to be here! If you want, I'll make three shelters as memorials—one for you, one for Moses, and one for Elijah."

[5] But even as he spoke, a bright cloud overshadowed them, and a voice from the cloud said, "This is my dearly loved Son, who brings me great joy. Listen to him." [6] The disciples were terrified and fell face down on the ground.

[7] Then Jesus came over and touched them. "Get up," he said. "Don't be afraid." (Matthew 17:1–7)

Peter, James, and John tremble at God the Father's voice. This is the same voice of the same God who asks Adam and Eve where they are hiding. Just like Adam and Eve, the three disciples are afraid—full of fear.

But look at Jesus.

He comes to them, like God came to Adam and Eve. He touches them, like God did to make Adam and Eve new clothes. And then what does Jesus say, right after God the Father tells them to listen to Him? *Do not be afraid.* That's the only proper response—following God the Father's command—to the world's first terrorist attack: *For us to not be afraid—and only because of Jesus.*

The War on Terror

The chamber falls silent, as one man stands at the podium preparing to deliver an address to a resilient nation, her allies, and her enemies that will mark a turning point in world history.

On September 20, 2001, only nine days after the terrorist attacks inflicted on American soil that we now familiarly call "Nine-Eleven" or simply "September 11th," President George W. Bush coined the term "War on Terror." In your mind, take yourself back to September 20, 2001. Time is the great mitigator of emotions. The intensity of our feelings dulls and fades as days turn to weeks, then to months, years, and decades. Try and remember the wide range and intensity of the emotions you felt—grief, mourning, numbness, disbelief, uncertainty, fear, anger, resiliency, determination, unity, hope—as you imagine listening to the following excerpts of President Bush's September 20, 2001, address:

> Our war on terror begins with Al Qaeda, but it does not end there.
>
> It will not end until every terrorist group of global reach has been found, stopped and defeated.
>
> Americans are asking, "Why do they hate us?"
>
> They hate what they see right here in this chamber: a democratically elected government. Their leaders are self-appointed. They hate our freedoms: our freedom of religion, our freedom of speech, our freedom to vote and assemble and disagree with each other. . . .
>
> These terrorists kill not merely to end lives, but to disrupt and end a way of life. With every atrocity, they hope that America grows fearful, retreating from the world and forsaking our friends. They stand against us because we stand in their way. . . .
>
> This is the world's fight. This is civilization's fight. This is the fight of all who believe in progress and pluralism, tolerance and freedom. . . .

> After all that has just passed, all the lives taken and all the possibilities and hopes that died with them, it is natural to wonder if America's future is one of fear. . . .
>
> Freedom and fear are at war. The advance of human freedom, the great achievement of our time and the great hope of every time, now depends on us.
>
> Our nation, this generation, will lift the dark threat of violence from our people and our future. We will rally the world to this cause by our efforts, by our courage. We will not tire, we will not falter and we will not fail. . . .
>
> The course of this conflict is not known, yet its outcome is certain. Freedom and fear, justice and cruelty, have always been at war, and we know that God is not neutral between them. . . .
>
> Fellow citizens, we'll meet violence with patient justice, assured of the rightness of our cause and confident of the victories to come.
>
> In all that lies before us, may God grant us wisdom and may he watch over the United States of America.

Thank God for not being neutral between fear and the freedom found in love! May God continue to grant us all wisdom today. Amen.

The War on Terror didn't begin on September 20, 2001, as President Bush said. It began the moment Satan and his angels were thrown down from heaven to earth. Like news networks reporting live in New York City, Washington, DC, and Somerset County, Pennsylvania, the Apostle John provides the equivalent of live reporting from eternity past in his apocalyptic vision recorded in the book of Revelation:

> Then there was war in heaven. Michael and his angels fought against the dragon and his angels.

[8] And the dragon lost the battle, and he and his angels were forced out of heaven. [9] This great dragon—the ancient serpent called the devil, or Satan, the one deceiving the whole world—was thrown down to the earth with all his angels.

[10] Then I heard a loud voice shouting across the heavens, "It has come at last—salvation and power and the Kingdom of our God, and the authority of his Christ. For the accuser of our brothers and sisters has been thrown down to earth—the one who accuses them before our God day and night. [11] And they have defeated him by the blood of the Lamb and by their testimony. And they did not love their lives so much that they were afraid to die. [12] Therefore, rejoice, O heavens! And you who live in the heavens, rejoice! But terror will come on the earth and the sea, for the devil has come down to you in great anger, knowing that he has little time."

[13a] When the dragon realized that he had been thrown down to the earth, he . . . [17b] declared war against the rest of her children—all who keep God's commandments and maintain their testimony for Jesus. (Revelation 12:7–13a, 17b)

Ah, the book of Revelation. One of the most talked about and confusing books of the Bible—misunderstood, mispreached, and misapplied. It is used by Satan to distract us from what really matters. How? Because we ask the wrong question when reading it. We ask *"When?"* instead of *"Who?"* The book of Revelation begins and ends with Jesus. It is the revelation of Jesus Christ that is meant to encourage His followers by communicating His assured victory and coming return.[7]

John's vision crystallizes this *spiritual war on terror*:

> And the dragon was angry at the woman and declared war against the rest of her children—all who keep God's commandments and maintain their testimony for Jesus. (Revelation 12:17)

Satan, in the symbolic form of a dragon, becomes so angry against the symbolic Mary—the human mother of Jesus Christ—that he declares war not only on Jesus but on the rest of her children. Who are these children? Followers of Jesus Christ—all who keep God's commandments and maintain their testimony for Him. Those who do not fear the consequences—from demeaning words meant to embarrass to demonic ways meant to kill—to ally with Jesus.

I call this a *spiritual war on terror* because the Apostle Paul clearly declares it to the early church in Ephesus:

> Finally, be strong in the Lord and in the strength of his might. [11] Put on the whole armor of God, that you may be able to stand against the schemes of the devil. [12] For we do not wrestle against flesh and blood, but against the rulers, against the authorities, against the cosmic powers over this present darkness, against the spiritual forces of evil in the heavenly places. [13] Therefore take up the whole armor of God, that you may be able to withstand in the evil day, and having done all, to stand firm. [14] Stand therefore, having fastened on the belt of truth, and having put on the breastplate of righteousness, [15] and, as shoes for your feet, having put

---

[7]   Revelation 1:1a: This is a revelation from Jesus Christ,
Revelation 22:20–21: He who is the faithful witness to all these things says, "Yes, I am coming soon!" Amen! Come, Lord Jesus! [21] May the grace of the Lord Jesus be with God's holy people.

on the readiness given by the gospel of peace. [16] In all circumstances take up the shield of faith, with which you can extinguish all the flaming darts of the evil one; [17] and take the helmet of salvation, and the sword of the Spirit, which is the word of God, (Ephesians 6:10–17 (ESV))

In our spiritual war on terror, we are fighting on three fronts:

1. **Against evil rulers and authorities of the unseen world, including Satan and his demonic army.** The Apostle Peter exhorts us in 1 Peter 5:8, "Stay alert! Watch out for your great enemy, the devil. He prowls around like a roaring lion, looking for someone to devour." The Apostle John sees Satan's army in his vision recorded in Revelation and provides the reason for Paul proclaiming that we will be standing firm after the battle.[8]

2. **Against mighty powers in this dark world, including those who believe and act contrary to the truth found in the gospel of Jesus Christ.** This battlefront includes people who don't believe there is any god and those who believe in and worship false gods. Their actions range from politely declining to talk about Jesus while thinking those who follow Him are "out of their minds," to outright verbal and physical persecution. Some spare no method of torture or murder toward those who identify with Jesus. Without a doubt, Satan inspires these mighty powers personified to wage war against followers of Jesus.

3. **Against evil spirits in the heavenly places.** This front may be the most difficult for us to comprehend. However, the prophet Daniel's inspired vision recorded in Daniel 10 sheds light on this battlefront:

---

[8] Revelation 20:9: And I saw them [Satan's army] as they went up on the broad plain of the earth and surrounded God's people and the beloved city. But fire from heaven came down on the attacking armies and consumed them.

I looked up and saw a man dressed in linen clothing, with a belt of pure gold around his waist. [6] His body looked like a precious gem. His face flashed like lightning, and his eyes flamed like torches. His arms and feet shone like polished bronze, and his voice roared like a vast multitude of people.

[7] Only I, Daniel, saw this vision. The men with me saw nothing, but they were suddenly terrified and ran away to hide. [8] So I was left there all alone to see this amazing vision. My strength left me, my face grew deathly pale, and I felt very weak. [9] Then I heard the man speak, and when I heard the sound of his voice, I fainted and lay there with my face to the ground.

[10] Just then a hand touched me and lifted me, still trembling, to my hands and knees. [11] And the man said to me, "Daniel, you are very precious to God, so listen carefully to what I have to say to you. Stand up, for I have been sent to you." When he said this to me, I stood up, still trembling.

[12] Then he said, "Don't be afraid, Daniel. Since the first day you began to pray for understanding and to humble yourself before your God, your request has been heard in heaven. I have come in answer to your prayer. [13] But for twenty-one days the spirit prince of the kingdom of Persia blocked my way. Then Michael, one of the archangels, came to help me, and I left him there with the spirit prince of the kingdom of Persia. [14] Now I am here to explain what will happen to your people in the future, for this vision concerns a time yet to come." (Daniel 10:5–14)

God sends an angel to answer Daniel's prayer, but the angel battles with an evil spirit for twenty-one days. Then, the archangel Michael arrives to the battle, providing the way for the first angel to declare God's answer to Daniel's prayer. Have you ever felt like God isn't listening or isn't there? Do the echoes of silence reverberate in your heart and mind? Do you sometimes doubt whether God really hears your prayers or sees you and the circumstances you face? Remember this battlefront and be encouraged.

You are precious to God. We are to stand up *unafraid* when we stand up humbly before Him. He knows what you've gone through, where you're at now, and where you're going. Take heart!

Specific clothing and uniforms often are used identify and protect those warriors in and out of battle. If we are battling in a spiritual war on three fronts, then what do we wear to identify and protect us? Preachers and authors, rightfully so, continue to go to great lengths to teach about the *full armor of God*. Paul describes the protective clothing we are to wear as we fight this spiritual war on terror: The belt of truth, the body armor of God's righteousness, the shoes of peace that comes from the gospel, the shield of faith, the helmet of salvation, and the sword of the Spirit (God's Word). At this point in our journey, we won't dive into detail about what we wear. Hopefully by the conclusion of our time together, though, we will instinctively understand and obediently wear the full armor of God to resist evil and, ultimately, stand firm in victory alongside Jesus.

In the meantime, may we be encouraged by Paul who writes in 2 Timothy 2:3, "Endure suffering along with me, as a good soldier of Christ Jesus." If you and I are like Paul, we want to be good soldiers of Jesus' army.

Your James 1:22 Challenge

James, the half-brother of Jesus Christ,[9] writes near the beginning of his letter to the early church:

> But don't just listen to God's word. You must do what it says. Otherwise, you are only fooling yourselves. (James 1:22)

Besides the teenage phase when almost all of us try to impress people by any means possible, do you know anybody who actually *wants* to be a fool? If all we do is read and listen to God's Word—and it doesn't impact us afterward—then something's wrong. Bluntly, we're being foolish. That's why I want to issue a *James 1:22 Challenge* at the end of each chapter.

While I am in no way claiming that this book is inspired, I purposefully base it heavily on God's inspired book, the Holy Bible. So, I want you to hear God's Word and believe it in your heart to the point where your life is transformed by the Holy Spirit and you think and act differently. If God uses this book to transform even one area of one person's heart and soul—just one life transformed—then praise Him! With that said, I am boldly praying and asking God to transform multitudes of lives so they are characterized by a desire to transform the world for God's kingdom and glory. May He be at work in and through you and me ever more so each and every day!

Take the *James 1:22 Challenge* by meditating on and praying over these questions and ideas with God in your heart:

1. Do you understand that we are caught in a spiritual battle between the One, True, Perfect, Holy, Living God and the evil Satan? God wants what is best for us. Satan wants what's best for him.

2. Have you been saved from the world's first terrorist attack by the efforts of the Ultimate First Responder, Jesus

---

[9] I wonder how many times James grumbled when his mother, Mary, rhetorically asked, "Why can't you just be more like your half-brother, Jesus?"

Christ, who was sent by God the Father because of His love for us? If you aren't sure where you stand with God or you aren't sure why Jesus died for you, please re-read Ephesians 6:10–17. The "helmet of salvation" is trusting in Jesus Christ as your Savior and Lord. We'll talk about this more in our next class. Please keep reading!

3. If you can answer yes to Question #2, are you acting in obedience to God when it comes to fear, allowing Him to care for both your short- and long-term needs?

4. Do you recognize that, as Christians, we are soldiers engaging in real battles as part of the spiritual war on terror? What are the three battlefronts we must be aware of as part of the war?

5. Write down some examples of the most vicious spiritual attacks and fights you've lived through, and try to identify how all three battlefronts identified in Question #4 played a role in those attacks. In other words, what do you find Satan tempting you with most often? In what areas do you find yourself continuing to fall prey to sin? How does it affect your relationship with yourself, with others, and with God?

Chapter 2:
History 102: The World's First
Knitting Project

"Nobody knows the real me. Nobody knows how many times I've sat in my room and cried, how many times I've lost hope, how many times I've been let down. Nobody knows how many times I've had to hold back the tears, how many times I've felt like I'm about to snap but don't just for the sake of others. Nobody knows the thoughts that have gone through my head whenever I'm sad, and how horrible they really are. Nobody. Knows. Me."
- Unknown

"You know what I am going to say even before I say it, LORD. You go before me and follow me. . . . How precious are your thoughts about me, O God. They cannot be numbered!"
- King David, Psalm 139:4–5a, 17

W hat logically follows a look at the world's first terrorist attack? A look at the world's first knitting project, of course![1] Actually, we'll be going *further* back in time in eternity past to see how God made us. It's digging back into eternity past to see how God creates and His creation that will help us understand more about who we are and who God is. We need to have this foundational background in history before we can move on

---

[1]   You know that's what you were thinking! From the front lines of war to the back rooms of yarn. Makes total sense. Don't question it; just keep reading!

41

to language, math, and biology. In fact, along with this important background, we'll then see a preview—a sneak peak of what's ahead—of a life marked by biblical fear.

To begin our second history lesson, join me as we listen to King Solomon's father, the giant-slaying King David, describe the world's first knitting project and exalt the Knitter:

> O LORD, you have examined my heart and know everything about me. [2] You know when I sit down or stand up. You know my thoughts even when I'm far away. [3] You see me when I travel and when I rest at home. You know everything I do. [4] You know what I am going to say even before I say it, LORD. [5] You go before me and follow me. You place your hand of blessing on my head. [6] Such knowledge is too wonderful for me, too great for me to understand!

> [7] I can never escape from your Spirit! I can never get away from your presence! [8] If I go up to heaven, you are there; if I go down to the grave, you are there. [9] If I ride the wings of the morning, if I dwell by the farthest oceans, [10] even there your hand will guide me, and your strength will support me. [11] I could ask the darkness to hide me and the light around me to become night—[12] but even in darkness I cannot hide from you. To you the night shines as bright as day. Darkness and light are the same to you.

> [13] You made all the delicate, inner parts of my body and knit me together in my mother's womb. [14] Thank you for making me so wonderfully complex! Your workmanship is marvelous—how well I know it. [15] You watched me as I was being formed in utter seclusion, as I was woven together in the dark of the womb. [16] You saw me before I

was born. Every day of my life was recorded in your book. Every moment was laid out before a single day had passed.

[17] How precious are your thoughts about me, O God. They cannot be numbered! [18] I can't even count them; they outnumber the grains of sand! And when I wake up, you are still with me!

[19] O God, if only you would destroy the wicked! Get out of my life, you murderers! [20] They blaspheme you; your enemies misuse your name. [21] O LORD, shouldn't I hate those who hate you? Shouldn't I despise those who oppose you? [22] Yes, I hate them with total hatred, for your enemies are my enemies.

[23] Search me, O God, and know my heart; test me and know my anxious thoughts. [24] Point out anything in me that offends you, and lead me along the path of everlasting life. (Psalm 139)

The psalms are lyrical works, like poems or songs, that the Israelites (or the Jewish nation) sang. All are inspired by God and are often full of raw emotions, from anger and grief to overflowing thankfulness and joy. One of the most famous Israelite kings is King David, and this psalm is one of his masterpieces. Together, let's look at five themes or ideas of this lyrical work.

God Knows

Who knows you so well that they know what you're thinking or what you're going to say before you say it? My wife, Kelly, can finish my thoughts before I even begin them! What am I ordering at the restaurant for dinner? Why, yes, it's the barbeque chicken. How did she know? What sweater am I wearing on this cold winter's day? Yes, the blue one with the zipper.[2] She did it again! Most likely, we all have someone like Kelly, whether it's our spouse or a close friend.

But, do you realize that whoever that person is pales in comparison to God? The original Hebrew language of the first six verses of Psalm 139 conveys the idea of God digging deep into the earth, where you and I come from, to investigate its roots—our innermost parts. David expands on this idea in verse 15, as we'll later see. God not only finishes your sentences or knows what you're going to wear, He knows them before you even think to speak or walk to the closet! Infinitely above finishing sentences or knowing outfits, God sees you as a valuable creation. At all times, in all situations, you are secured and enclosed by God. He knows everything—including everything about you—and *desires* to guide and protect you.

Time out! Let that soak in. God knows us in such an intimate way and, armed with that knowledge, loves us so much that He encircles us with His protection and blessing. Does this make you in awe like David? We'll see in language class that being in awe of God, as David is here, is a form of biblically fearing God.

Yup, *fearing*.

God Goes

When you think about spiritual ideas—like fear—have you ever become overwhelmed? For example, asking yourself if God is *actually* real? Does He *really* know everything? How can our spirit actually be someplace *forever*, for all eternity? These are all perfectly acceptable questions for Christians to ask on this side of Heaven. That's why we have what's known as faith, described in Hebrews 11:1: "Faith shows the reality of what we hope for; it is the evidence of things we cannot see."

David's first reaction to the idea that God is all-knowing— what he describes in the first six verses—is being overwhelmed. We see this in verses 7–12. If God has such intimate knowledge

---

[2] I only own blue sweaters. There's variety, though. Some have zippers. One even has a small maroon stripe. No joke: I still wear the sweater I was wearing in our church directory photo—when I was in college a decade earlier.

of us and His creation, David concludes that he cannot escape God. From the heights of heaven to the depths of the earth, from the dawn in the east to the dusk in the west, God goes with you. Because of God's grace, the darkness of your sin can't stop the light of a holy God. Do you believe it? I don't mean just knowing it as an intellectual fact. I mean experiencing the awe-striking reality to the point it changes the way you think, feel, and act.

Have you experienced Jesus' "give and take" in your life? Has He taken the penalty for your sins onto Himself and, at the same time, given you His righteousness? Talk about the most unfair trade in all of eternity that's overflowing of grace and mercy.

Imagine if it were a draft day trade in a sports league. God, as the Owner-Commissioner, walks to the podium and says, "And now, with humanity on the clock, we have a trade to announce!" *The crowd gasps before growing silent.*[3] "The trade is between Jesus Christ and all those who will believe in His death and resurrection." *The crowd murmurs, and media analysts are already trying to analyze what they don't even know.*[4] "Jesus Christ receives death—the penalty for humanity's sins." *Shock overcomes the crowd as God continues to speak.* "In return, those who will follow Jesus as their Lord and Savior will receive Jesus' righteousness."

Analysts are going crazy while looking at this trade! *Surely, there's some future considerations that humanity will have to give God.* They seek clarification and receive confirmation that there are no other components of the deal. *The trade is so lopsided toward those who will believe in Jesus because it's truly a gift from God. It's so full of mercy and grace. God, in His mercy, withholds the just punishment for our sins—death. And, in His grace, God gives us what we don't deserve—Jesus Christ's righteousness. Yet, because God is just, He doles out the punishment for humanity's sin—death—onto His own Son, Jesus.*

Each of us has a choice to accept this gift from God. If you and I accept by following Jesus as our Savior and Lord, then God the

---

[3] New York Jets fans are still booing, because that's what they do at the draft regardless of what's happening.

[4] Mel Kiper, Jr., doesn't even have this on his draft board. It's *that* shocking.

Father sees His Son's righteousness—and not your or my sins—when He looks at us. What does He see when He looks at you? If God the Father sees God the Son's righteousness, talk about awe-inspiring!

If you can't say you've truly accepted this free gift even if you claim to be a Christian, I hope and pray you will talk to a Christian friend. No single more important decision that you will make is more important than choosing to follow Jesus, accepting Him as your personal Savior and Lord. There's nothing we can do to save ourselves. We bring nothing to the draft-day trade. Instead, we bring sinful selves and accept the free gift of adoption as God's sons and daughters through Jesus Christ, and Him alone. You can always come back to finish this book and, trust me, it will make a lot more sense with the Holy Spirit—who indwells in your heart once you choose to follow Jesus—guiding your life!

Son or daughter of God, it's that awe-inspiring feeling David describes that we'll soon see is biblical *fear.*

God Sews

Her favorite rocking chair slowly and smoothly moves back and forth amidst a myriad, or a proverbial rainbow, of different colored yarns balled together on the floor. A couple of strands trace their way up from the floor, surviving the batting of cats' paws, over the armrest, and onto the needles being maneuvered with the skill of a surgeon, with lightning fast, accurate movements. The strands come together in the latest stitch of the knitter's latest creation—her handiwork.

Sound familiar? Do you have someone in your own life that this describes?

I have never seen someone sew and knit as much as Stella Morgan, who is like family to me. Her fingers never stop! Open heart surgery didn't slow her down. Neither did multiple surgeries on her carotid arteries. Nonstop pain from arthritis doesn't slow her down. Nothing keeps her from her crafting. Whether it's blankets for those less fortunate to keep warm, scarves for friends to be fashionable, lace doilies to set the table for a holiday meal, or 200 feet of cloth triangles to be stretched from rows of trees as a banner for an outdoor wedding—she knits, and sews, and then knits some more. She has so many different types of needles that an acupuncturist would be jealous!

When you take the time to watch someone sit down with a couple of knitting needles and yarn in-hand to set to work, you can be mesmerized as the creator makes one intricate movement after another, meticulously following a plan to create something beautiful. Now think about the picture David paints of God's miraculous and wondrous work inside an expectant mother. Close your eyes and think of God knitting together each strand of your DNA that then shapes your body and being. From bones and muscles to a brain and beating heart, the Almighty God creates a living being inside another in the image of Him. And, because God is all-knowing and all-present, He sees the finished product—each day you live—even before He starts sewing.

You were made intentionally by the True God who loves you. Some English translations of the original Hebrew say that we were *fearfully* made. Without skipping ahead to language class, this is the same awe-inspiring reverence that we just talked about. Like before, David reverently cries out as he esteems God's work and thoughts.

Are God's work and thoughts as precious to you as they are to David?

God's Foes

"You're either with us or against us!" Does that phrase sound familiar? From teenage fights to political mudslinging, this exclamation immediately divides the audience into two camps. There's no middle ground, no riding the fence. You choose to support the one exclaiming the phrase, or your lack of support is interpreted as a sign of downright opposition.

Perhaps no greater exclamation of this phrase can be found than in the gospels of Matthew and Luke that record Jesus saying this to a crowd after He casts out a demon.[5] David takes a page

---

[5]   Matthew 12:30 and Luke 11:23: "Anyone who isn't with me opposes me, and anyone who isn't working with me is actually working against me."

out of Jesus' playbook almost 1,000 years prior, as he transitions from describing his fearful awe of the All-Knowing, All-Present God to lashing out against those enemies who are far away from God. David's response to God's call and of being close to Him is clear: If you're an enemy of God, then you're an enemy of him.

If you have responded to God's free gift of Jesus' "give and take," you live by faith in Jesus. God creates in you the desire to grow closer to Him. His Holy Spirit searches out sin in you that inhibits your walk with Him and convicts you of it. In the same way, you see sin that separates you from God with a loathsome hatred. You live out James 4:8–9, by toiling heavily, enduring laborious hardships, weeping, and feeling miserable because of a deep affliction of your sin.[6] It is easy for even the most maturing Christian to become lax when it comes to comprehending fully and recognizing the gravity of our sin to a holy and righteous God. Armed with that knowledge, you are an ambassador of God, extending His love to sinners as you recognize deeper and deeper levels of the grace shown to you from God. You are a reconciled reconciler, being used by God—while He continues to work in you—to draw others to Him in His Spirit (see 2 Corinthians 5:17–21).[7]

As we progress through more classes and into the Lab of Life, we'll begin to understand more of David's expression of allegiance to God. It's with this allegiance that we pledge dis-allegiance to anything contrary to Him. While we're only previewing the idea

---

[6] James 4:8–9: Come close to God, and God will come close to you. Wash your hands, you sinners; purify your hearts, for your loyalty is divided between God and the world. [9] Let there be tears for what you have done. Let there be sorrow and deep grief. Let there be sadness instead of laughter, and gloom instead of joy.

[7] 2 Corinthians 5:17–21 (ESV): Therefore, if anyone is in Christ, he is a new creation. The old has passed away; behold, the new has come. [18] All this is from God, who through Christ reconciled us to himself and gave us the ministry of reconciliation; [19] that is, in Christ God was reconciling the world to himself, not counting their trespasses against them, and entrusting to us the message of reconciliation. [20] Therefore, we are ambassadors for Christ, God making his appeal through us. We implore you on behalf of Christ, be reconciled to God. [21] For our sake he made him to be sin who knew no sin, so that in him we might become the righteousness of God.

now in history class, know that as our fear of God increases, so does our hatred of the enemy, Satan, and his weapon, sin.

God Shows

A hypocrite: We've all seen one—we've all been one. Someone who says one thing then acts in exactly the opposite manner. It's the living equivalent of realizing your favorite purse or your favorite athlete's autographed jersey is a knockoff, fake, phony, not the real thing, and worth nothing compared to the real and authentic.

After taking a stand against God's enemies and calling for their defeat, David asks God for a gut-check (or, more aptly, a spirit-check). David wants his life to be marked not by hypocrisy but with integrity. If he publicly claims to walk closely with God, he wants privately to be doing so. Walking the talk. If you are a Christian, yet are living a hypocritical life that doesn't display fruits of the Spirit (see Galatians 5:22–23),[8] then you are pointing people away from God and not toward Him. The inauthenticity and hypocrisy of contemporary, cultural Christianity leaves a watching world calloused toward Christ.

Note how David concludes asking God to search him—the same action he extols in the very first verse of this psalm. David returns to where he began, asking God to reveal and show anything for which he needs to repent. It's through repentance that we are led by God. It's through repentance that truth replaces fraud and the authentic replaces the hypocrite. It's through repentance that the world sees Jesus in and through us. And, as we'll soon see, it's through repentance and obedience that we *fear* God.

Your James 1:22 Challenge

James writes to us, "But don't just listen to God's word. You must do what it says. Otherwise, you are only fooling yourselves." Use the following five prompts to apply lessons learned from this chapter centered on God's Word to transform your life.

---

[8] Galatians 5:22–23a (ESV): But the fruit of the Spirit is love, joy, peace, patience, kindness, goodness, faithfulness, [23] gentleness, self-control;

1. Prayerfully ask God to create in you the desire to know and experience Him like David does.

2. Remember that wherever you go, God will be with you.

3. See your body, personality, and life as God's handiwork.

4. Recognize the enemy in God's battle, and be Jesus' authentic ambassador to others.

5. Ask God to show you anything for which you need to repent and seek His forgiveness in grace, and then be led by Him to live authentically and with integrity.

Chapter 3:
Language 101: What Does It Mean to Biblically Fear God?

"I've been listening, and reading, and pouring over the Word of God and praying and crying and laughing to [God] for fifteen years of my life now. And I have never been so unsure and scared and doubtful than I am right now, in my early 20s."
-    A person's post on an online Christian message board

"This means that anyone who belongs to Christ has become a new person. The old life is gone; a new life has begun! And all of this is a gift from God, who brought us back to himself through Christ. And God has given us this task of reconciling people to him."
-    The Apostle Paul, 2 Corinthians 5:17–18

Having been around for thousands of years, it was first made famous in American pop culture by Charlie Brown's teacher. It is the constant, incessant droning of someone talking about what may or may not be important. For whatever reason, you just don't care. Maybe you're tired like Eutychus,[1] or maybe you are thinking about something that is more important to you. Someone is rambling on and on, and you've basically checked out. Maybe you're a student, and it's just one of those days where what the

---

[1] If you don't know who Eutychus is, check out Acts 20:9 (ESV): "And a young man named Eutychus, sitting at the window, sank into a deep sleep as Paul talked still longer. And being overcome by sleep, he fell down from the third story and was taken up dead." Don't worry, he miraculously ends up living!

teacher says just isn't sticking in your mind. Regardless of the different details, one thing remains in common: There's no clear communication occurring because you either don't think what the person is saying has any relevance to you, or you simply don't understand what in the world they're talking about.

This can easily be applied to you and me sitting in church listening to a sermon.[2] We've all been there. What's being taught and how it's being communicated simply doesn't seem applicable to your life, with all that you're going through. Or, you may simply have no idea what the preacher or teacher is talking about. Someone is dropping theological bombs as if they're preaching their seminary dissertation, and you're caught right in the middle of it, thinking about something else. Whether it's an upcoming school project, a deadline at work, the putt you missed during yesterday's golf game, how that lady three rows down is wearing the same dress you are, or the Internet site that streams pictures of people terrified in a haunted house, you simply aren't listening.

You're thinking about anything else than what's being said. I pray that today is not one of those days as you continue to read this book. Please take your time and reduce your speed for the theological construction zone ahead. Once you get through it, you'll have a solid foundation of what it means to fear God.

Fear What?

Did you know that in the original languages of the biblical manuscripts, ten Hebrew words and phrases plus eleven Greek words and phrases are used to describe what is translated as "fear" in English? Additionally, depending on the Bible translation, the word "fear" is used between 350 and 550 times.

Here's where it gets even trickier. Stay with me now. The word translated "fear" in many versions of the Bible comes from a Hebrew word that has a range of meaning in the Scriptures. Sometimes it refers to the fear we feel in anticipation of some danger or pain, but it can also mean a feeling of awe or reverence.

---

[2] Or reading a book, except for this one.

Also built into the definition in the original language are the ideas of wonder, amazement, mystery, astonishment, gratitude, admiration, and worship. Think about David's reaction to God that we saw in the last chapter.

Fearing God then includes an overwhelming sense of the glory, worth, and beauty of God. God, through His prophet Jeremiah, asks Israel sometime around 600 BC and us today:

> Do you not fear me? . . . Do you not tremble before
> me? I placed the sand as the boundary for the sea,
> a perpetual barrier that it cannot pass; though the
> waves toss, they cannot prevail; though they roar,
> they cannot pass over it. (Jeremiah 5:22 (ESV))

Does your knowledge of God and faith in Him cause you to tremble in respect toward Him? But that still begs the question: *How do we biblically fear God?*

Fear This

In this language class, we'll discover the four steps to fearing God in a biblical sense. We'll be going back and forth between two of the Apostle Paul's letters. The first will be his letter to the Romans, while the second is to the early church in the city of Ephesus. Specifically, we'll be listening to Paul's words in Romans 3:9–31, where Paul is writing to the early church in Rome that is made up of both Jews and Gentiles (non-Jewish followers of Christ). Some controversy is brewing about how the two groups of people are to come together under one church as followers of Jesus. Paul conveys similar ideas in his letter to the Ephesians.

Before we dive into God's Word, I want to give you a head start and share with you the four steps to fearing God biblically. We fear God by:

1. Seeing who we are.
2. Seeing who God is.
3. Believing what God has done, is doing, and will do.

4. Responding in obedience to God.

First, we see who we are. Second, we see who God is. Third, we believe what God has done in the past, is doing in the present (including right now even as you read this!), and will do in the future and for all eternity. Finally, all three of those steps shape how we respond in obedience to God.

Join me in Romans 3, beginning in verse 9. As we read Paul's God-inspired words to the Romans and to us, be on the lookout for the four steps to biblically fearing God.

> Well then, should we conclude that we Jews are better than others? No, not at all, for we have already shown that all people, whether Jews or Gentiles, are under the power of sin. [10] As the Scriptures say, "No one is righteous—not even one. [11] No one is truly wise; no one is seeking God. [12] All have turned away; all have become useless. No one does good, not a single one." [13] "Their talk is foul, like the stench from an open grave. Their tongues are filled with lies." "Snake venom drips from their lips." [14] "Their mouths are full of cursing and bitterness." [15] "They rush to commit murder. [16] Destruction and misery always follow them. [17] They don't know where to find peace." [18] "They have no fear of God at all."
>
> [19] Obviously, the law applies to those to whom it was given, for its purpose is to keep people from having excuses, and to show that the entire world is guilty before God. [20] For no one can ever be made right with God by doing what the law commands. The law simply shows us how sinful we are.
>
> [21] But now God has shown us a way to be made right with him without keeping the requirements

of the law, as was promised in the writings of Moses and the prophets long ago. [22] We are made right with God by placing our faith in Jesus Christ. And this is true for everyone who believes, no matter who we are.

[23] For everyone has sinned; we all fall short of God's glorious standard. [24] Yet God, in his grace, freely makes us right in his sight. He did this through Christ Jesus when he freed us from the penalty for our sins. [25] For God presented Jesus as the sacrifice for sin. People are made right with God when they believe that Jesus sacrificed his life, shedding his blood. This sacrifice shows that God was being fair when he held back and did not punish those who sinned in times past, [26] for he was looking ahead and including them in what he would do in this present time. God did this to demonstrate his righteousness, for he himself is fair and just, and he declares sinners right in his sight when they believe in Jesus.

[27] Can we boast, then, that we have done anything to be accepted by God? No, because our acquittal is not based on obeying the law. It is based on faith. [28] So we are made right with God through faith and not by obeying the law.

[29] After all, is God the God of the Jews only? Isn't he also the God of the Gentiles? Of course he is. [30] There is only one God, and he makes people right with himself only by faith, whether they are Jews or Gentiles. [31] Well then, if we emphasize faith, does this mean that we can forget about the law? Of course not! In fact, only when we have faith do we truly fulfill the law. (Romans 3:9–31)

Wow, that's a lot to take in! We could spend pages upon pages and books upon books on this passage.

For now, first simply pay special attention to this phrase in verse 18: "They have no *fear* of God at all" (emphasis added). Second, pay special attention to the first word in verse 21. It's so important. Given all that Paul just says describing us, the simple three-letter word "but" provides hope for the hopeless. Despite everything that Paul describes of Jews, Gentiles, and us today, God has a plan!

Before we dive further into it, though, let's jump over to the second chapter of Paul's letter to the Ephesians. Note the familiarity between Paul's writing to the church in Rome and now to the church in Ephesus, and keep in mind the four steps to fearing God biblically.[3]

> Once you were dead because of your disobedience and your many sins. ² You used to live in sin, just like the rest of the world, obeying the devil—the commander of the powers in the unseen world. He is the spirit at work in the hearts of those who refuse to obey God. ³ All of us used to live that way, following the passionate desires and inclinations of our sinful nature. By our very nature we were subject to God's anger, just like everyone else.
>
> ⁴ But God is so rich in mercy, and he loved us so much, ⁵ that even though we were dead because of our sins, he gave us life when he raised Christ from the dead. (It is only by God's grace that you have been saved!) ⁶ For he raised us from the dead along with Christ and seated us with him in the heavenly realms because we are united with Christ Jesus. ⁷ So God can point to us in all future ages as examples of the incredible wealth of his

---

[3] Remember: First, seeing who we are. Second, seeing who God is. Third, believing what God has done, is doing, and will do. And, finally, responding in obedience to God.

grace and kindness toward us, as shown in all he
has done for us who are united with Christ Jesus.

[8] God saved you by his grace when you believed.
And you can't take credit for this; it is a gift from
God. Salvation is not a reward for the good things
we have done, so none of us can boast about it. [10]
For we are God's masterpiece. He has created us
anew in Christ Jesus, so we can do the good things
he planned for us long ago. (Ephesians 2:1–10)

Yet again, that's some heady theological bombs Paul is dropping on the church. He isn't mincing words, either. It's from these
passages that we can see how we are to fear God biblically.

Seeing Who We Are

Let's start with the first step to fearing God biblically. We first
fear God by seeing who we are. First and foremost, we are dead
in sin as victims of the world's first terrorist attack orchestrated
by Satan in his war against God. While we all may be alive physically, we are all dead spiritually because of Adam and Eve's falling
to Satan's temptation. Paul echoes this thought emphatically by
saying in both Ephesians 2:1 and Romans 3:9–10 that, at one time,
all of us were dead because of our sin.

What does it mean to be "dead in sin?" How do we become
dead in our sin? It's actually pretty frightening in and of itself to
realize, as Paul explains in Ephesians 2:2 and Romans 3:12–18.
Literally, we are *obedient to the Devil* and *disobedient to God*.
Look at what Paul says in Ephesians 2:2: "You used to live in sin,
just like the rest of the world, obeying the devil—the commander
of the powers in the unseen world. He is the spirit at work in the
hearts of those who refuse to obey God."

That's just the executive summary, the shorter version. The
longer version is found in Romans 3:

All have turned away; all have become useless.
No one does good, not a single one." [13] "Their
talk is foul, like the stench from an open grave.
Their tongues are filled with lies." "Snake venom
drips from their lips." [14] "Their mouths are full of
cursing and bitterness."

[15] "They rush to commit murder. [16] Destruction
and misery always follow them. [17] They don't
know where to find peace." [18] "They have no fear
of God at all." (Romans 3:12–18)

These can easily be just words on a page to us as we read
them. We can read them and think they don't apply to us. Foul
talk? Maybe some foul breath that smells like the stench from a
grave,[4] but not foul talk. Our tongues filled with lies? Maybe just
a white lie here or there. That snake venom language seems a little
strong, doesn't it? I mean, I don't see us all rushing out to commit
murder. However, this language applies to me, and it applies to you.
It applies to us all, and I want to make it personal to us. Each one
of us, as a human being, is born with a sinful nature that literally
makes us obedient to the Devil and disobedient to God.

Imagine a balloon, for example. Make it be your favorite color
and blow it up for all to see. As you hold this balloon, I want you to
let it represent God's perfect law. Earlier in his letter to the Romans
in chapter 2, verse 15, Paul writes that God's law is written on all
our hearts. Basically, he's saying we have no excuse when it comes
to knowing God's law, which is a reflection of God's character and
glory. It is holy, perfect, and just. Later on in Romans 3:19–20,
Paul writes that the law makes us all accountable to God because
it makes us aware of sin and its effects (my paraphrase).

Again, think of this balloon as God's law. Now, imagine all of
a sudden you see something being written on the balloon in big
black letters: MURDER. *Talk about a sin!* You may be thinking that
it can't get much "worse" than that. What happens when someone

---

[4] Mint, anyone?

commits murder? They are breaking God's law. *POP!* The balloon just burst. The murderer violates God's perfect law. You're likely thinking, "I'm not a murderer." Well, James writes in letter to the church, "For the person who keeps all of the laws except one is as guilty as a person who has broken all of God's laws" (James 2:10).

In other words, if you violate God's law in one area, you violate His entire law. No take-backs. Period. End of story. If we sin and are disobedient to God's law, we break it. We may think some sins are "bigger" or "worse" than others, but to a perfect God, they are all the same. They all result in the same thing: God's perfect law being broken.

So, instead of MURDER, the word LYING appears on the balloon.[5] *POP!*

GOSSIPING.[6] *POP!*

LUSTING AT PORNOGRAPHY.[7] *POP!*

PRIDEFUL JUDGING.[8] *POP!*

FUDGING YOUR BUSINESS NUMBERS OR YOUR TAXES.[9] *POP!*

CHEATING ON A TEST.[10] *POP!*

---

[5]   Even that little white lie you told that you can't even remember now. I know, I know, it seemed so insignificant at the time.

[6]   But you were just asking around so you could pray for them. We know.

[7]   It is scary what can be found on the Internet. I know from experience. Praise God for His grace and forgiveness!

[8]   Let compassion and grace fill the void left in the wake of not judging!

[9]   You may think you're doing it for your family's sake, but, in the end, it's not worth it.

[10] The Lord will get you in the school He wants you to be in regardless of a test score.

DISOBEYING YOUR PARENTS.[11] *POP!*

PUTTING ANYTHING BEFORE GOD AT ANY TIME IN YOUR LIFE.[12] *POP!*

Let the sound of balloons bursting resonate in your heart. *POP! POP! POP! POP!*

God's perfect, holy, just law being broken. *POP! POP! POP! POP!*

What's the result of our obedience to the Devil and being in dead in sin? Being disobedient to God and breaking His law. All of us—you and I—have broken God's law. That is who we are. Sin makes us fall short. Period. Nothing more than a pile of broken balloons, falling short of God's perfect, holy character and standard.

This logically leads to the third point that Paul points out about us in Ephesians 2:3. If these broken balloons represent our violation and breaking of God's law, then we are all subject to God's anger and wrath for eternity. If we stop here, trying to somehow grasp at a monstrous pile of busted balloon pieces and knowing we are subject to God's wrath, we have nothing to live for. We have nothing to hope for. That's just who we are. However, seeing who we are is only the beginning of the process.

Seeing Who God Is

After we see who we are, we then see who God is. That's the second step to fearing God biblically. And, it changes *everything*.

The first fact we need to know about God, as He reacts to those broken balloons—our sins, our disobedience of His law—is that He is righteous, fair, and just. You can see this in Romans 3:26.[13] This means that it would be inconsistent and incongruent with

---

[11] Talk about a catch-all.

[12] The catch-all of catch-alls. It's called idolatry. And, we all have idols. If you don't think you do, then one of your idols is yourself. Sorry.

[13] Excerpt from Romans 3:26: God did this to demonstrate his righteousness, for he himself is fair and just.

God's perfect nature *not* to punish those who break his law. He is a holy God who cannot sit idle when His law—His character—is stained by sin. It is because of His righteousness that He *must* hold accountable those who break His law, which is all of humanity, including you and me. Paul tells us in the first part of Romans 6:23 that sin's penalty is death.[14] God must put sin to death because of His holy and just character.

Conjunctions[15] play an important role in language, and certain conjunctions in the Bible have eternal ramifications. Conjunctions connect words, phrases, or ideas. Conjunctions tie them together in some way, making them relatable to one another. They can distinguish similarities or can be markers of difference. In the case of the conjunction "but," it's used in the English language to convey the idea that in spite of whatever the first thought is, the second thought will be of a marked difference.

We first noted the conjunction "but" in Romans 3:21, and we see the same word again at the beginning of Ephesians 2:4. It's in that simple, three-letter conjunction that God reveals more of His character. Because He is a God of grace and mercy, despite who we are, God doesn't change who He is. He sets in plan a motion that separates sin from Him while saving us in Him.

Paul's descriptors of God in Ephesians 2:4 and 2:7 give us all hope. If God wasn't merciful and loving as described in Ephesians 2:4, then He would not hold back the punishment that we all deserve for breaking His law. Mercy is withholding judgment on someone who deserves it. And, God does just this: He withholds His righteous anger toward us because He loves us. *He withholds because He loves.* Additionally, God is full of grace and kindness. In His kindness as described in Ephesians 2:7, God gives us something we don't deserve. That's what grace is—receiving something we don't deserve. *He gives because He loves.* In His mercy, God withholds what we rightfully deserve as punishment and, instead, in His grace, gives us what we don't rightfully deserve.

---

[14] Romans 6:23a (ESV): For the wages of sin is death,

[15] Conjunction junction, what's your function?

Believing What God Has Done, Is Doing, and Will Do

We unpack this thought further in our third step of biblically fearing God: Believing what God has done, what He is doing, and what He will do. It's this monumental, heaven- and earth-shattering fact that differentiates Christian hope from all other world religions. Look at Paul's words in Romans 3:24–25a: "Yet [despite all of us being obedient to the Devil and breaking God's law] God, in his grace, freely makes us right in his sight. He did this through Christ Jesus when he freed us from the penalty for our sins. For God presented Jesus as the sacrifice for sin. People are made right with God when they believe that Jesus sacrificed his life, shedding his blood."

God sacrificed His Son, Jesus, to pay the penalty for our sin. That's the gospel. That's *the* purpose for life. That's hope. That's God knitting together the rainbow pile of shattered rubber pieces with heavenly helium to restore the balloons we busted back into their original, perfect form. All of what God mercifully withheld from us, He poured out on Jesus. Jesus, through the shedding of His blood on the cross, took your penalty and He took my penalty for sinning. He took the penalty of all those who lived before us and all those not yet born. That's the gospel of Jesus Christ. That's the scandal of grace: Heavenly helium.

Notice, though, how I said this third step involves *believing*. It's only if we believe or place our faith in Jesus that God declares us right with Him. That's the second action God takes. He declares those who place their faith in Jesus right with Him according to Romans 3:26. Paul describes this miraculous action, using different language in Ephesians 2:6, which reads: "For he raised us from the dead along with Christ and seated us with him in the heavenly realms because we are united with Christ Jesus." Pause again and soak it in: *God raises us to life, united with Jesus Christ.*

In a nutshell, here's what God has done, is doing, and will do: While we are dead in sin, God mercifully withholds judgment on us; and, instead, He sacrifices His only Son, Jesus, to raise us to life, united with Christ, all because of His grace. That's Christianity.

That's what Christians hold their hope to. It's that transcending truth that's transforming lives.

You can't save yourself. You can only believe on the One who can, Jesus Christ.

Responding in Obedience to God

So far, we've seen that we biblically fear God by first seeing who we are; then seeing who God is; and believing what He has done, is doing, and will do. This brings us to our response to these actions.

We often quote King Solomon's exhortation:

> Trust in the Lord with all your heart; do not depend
> on your own understanding. [6] Seek his will in all
> you do, and he will show you which path to take.
> (Proverbs 3:5–6)

Look at the action verbs in these verses. We are commanded to *trust* God and to *seek* His will. You cannot passively *trust* or passively *seek*. It requires action. Hence, the fourth and final step to fearing God biblically is responding in obedience to God.

I want to be emphatically clear on this point. This is where we can misinterpret, misapply, and mislead, even with the best of intentions. Our obedience comes in response to what God has done for us and in us. The order is of paramount importance. It's not that we obey and then God saves. God saves—then we obey. Paul stresses this idea in Philippians 2:12–13 and Ephesians 2:8 when he emphasizes that God saves us in His grace when we believe. Grace and faith are gifts that can't be earned. Our obedience cannot earn what grace and faith give.

Our obedient response is not to earn grace. Instead, God acted in His grace so we could then please and glorify Him by living a life of faith in obedience that He Himself empowers us to live. Paul exhorts the early church in Philippi and us, writing:

> Dear friends, you always followed my instructions
> when I was with you. And now that I am away, it
> is even more important. Work hard to show the
> results of your salvation, obeying God with deep
> reverence and fear. [13] For God is working in you,
> giving you the desire and the power to do what
> pleases him. (Philippians 2:12–13)

Elaborating on the same theme to the Ephesian church and us, Paul writes:

> For we are God's masterpiece. He has created us
> anew in Christ Jesus, so we can do the good things
> he planned for us long ago. (Ephesians 2:10)

Our obedient response is God's Holy Spirit working in us, ever-conforming us be His *masterpiece*. I love the New Living Translation's choice of the word "masterpiece." In my millennial mind, it conveys so much more than the more common translation of "workmanship." A masterpiece is the best of an artist or creator's work. You and I, in Christ, are God's best work. More beautiful than the most beautiful thing in nature—the multi-colored sea shell, the most exotic wildlife area, the colorful hues of a picturesque sunset or of a double rainbow, the rolling mountains upon mountains painted with striking colors of fall leaves, the brilliant radiance of celestial stars and supernovas—You and I, in Christ, are more beautiful in God's eyes because we are made in His image. *You and I, in Christ, are God's best creation.*

John Parsons, a Hebrew scholar, describes this line of thinking as "a profound reverence for life that comes from rightly seeing. This level discerns the Presence of God in all things and is sometimes called . . . the 'Awe of the Exalted.' Through it we behold God's glory and majesty in all things. 'Fearing' and 'seeing' are linked and united. We are elevated to the level of reverent awareness, holy affection, and genuine communion with God's Holy Spirit."

Seeing works of artists full of creative talents amazes me. Aside for a little bit of musical ability[16] and the ability to draw a two-point perspective drawing,[17] my right brain is pretty plain. That's why I am often astonished at works of art. For example, imagine my awe when I came across a life-sized balloon bride.[18] Not a balloon animal, but a balloon human. Not just any balloon human, but a life-sized female balloon human in a white wedding dress with a veil and bouquet ready to be wed to her unseen balloon husband.

Seeing the work of art wasn't the most amazing thing, though. Do you know what I think is most amazing? Most life-altering? Most hope-filling? Most awe-inspiring? *Most fear-provoking?* It's recognizing that biblically fearing God means understanding and responding to the truth that the living God takes us and our piles of *POPPED!* balloons—the very pieces of balloons that represent our disobedience to His law—and *transforms us into the bride of Jesus Christ*, whom He sacrificed for you and for me.

He is taking us from a pile of nothing, deserving death, to a brilliant, radiant bride wed for all eternity to God. Now, that's what I call amazing! And, it's what inspires me to be in awe of God, revere Him, and—ultimately—*fear Him.*

Your James 1:22 Challenge

James writes to us, "But don't just listen to God's word. You must do what it says. Otherwise, you are only fooling yourselves." Use the following five prompts to apply lessons learned from this chapter centered on God's Word to transform your life.

1. Memorize our four-step definition for biblically fearing God:

   1) Seeing who you are.

---

[16] Proud "band geek" here!

[17] Because it's just straight lines.

[18] On the Internet, of course! I was probably procrastinating.

2) Seeing who God is.
3) Believing what He has done, is doing, and will do.
4) Responding in obedience to Him.

2. Are you walking in obedience? If yes, are you trying to earn grace, or is God transforming you into His masterpiece?

3. What sins have been *POPPING!* balloons in your life? Confess them, repent, and find an accountability partner to walk with you in the struggle.

4. Recognize that the global, corporate church is the hands and feet of Jesus today, and His bride for all eternity.

5. What beautiful creation inspires you to see God? Do you have a special place where your heart worships God? The beach? The mountains? How do you see God there?

Chapter 4:
Language 102: What Does It Mean to Live in a Fear-Full World?

"I don't know what's right and what's real anymore . . . 'cause I'm being taken over by the fear."
- Lily Allen, popular English singer, songwriter, and actress

"Where is your faith?"
- Jesus, to His disciples before calming the storm threatening their lives, Luke 8:25

Tiny beads of water begin to bubble up on his forehead, as Marty—a recent college graduate—stares across a bistro table from the sales agent "helping" him through the most important purchase of his first adult-magnitude decision of his life. Only his signature on a tablet separates him from a contract that will tie him down for multiple years to an asset that he will use every day to survive in today's America. No, Marty the Millennial is not afraid of committing to a mortgage, but to a digital telecommunications company. We're not talking the four walls of a house in one part of the world, we're talking about the unseen network that connects the world.

Why is Marty so fearful of what, to some, may be an ultimately trivial decision? Because he's like the average *Millennial*—one of the names given to those born roughly between the early 1980s and early 2000s. Saddled with almost $30,000 in student loan debt used to pay for a degree in one of the most competitive job markets in history with three generations vying for one generation's worth of jobs, Marty wonders if he can afford what he needs to thrive in today's market. He can't even afford to rent, so he's back in his high-school bedroom like one of out of three of his friends. That's why Millennials are also called *The Boomerang Generation.* They are sent out from home at the end of adolescence only to return home at the beginning of adulthood.

Another name for Millennials? *The Selfie Generation. The Generation of the Self.* Tuck this title away in the back of your mind for later classes. A lesser known, but perhaps the most descriptive name of Marty and his peers is *Generation Fear.* Bill Bergman, president and CEO of the Bergman Group and instructor of Marketing at the University of Richmond Robins School of Business, helps us understand more about Gene*ration Fear.*[1] Discussing the recent trend of his students being marked by timidity, reluctance, and *fear,* Bergman recounts:

> When I finally asked . . . what was wrong, they told me they were nervous about saying anything too contentious because they feared it would be broadcast across social media. . . . Digital connectivity seems to be ratcheting up the anxiety factor. These kids never unplug and it is slowly driving them crazy. Social media platforms may be even more powerful than the fear of violence. . . . At age 22 it's painful enough managing your real self, much less the addition of a full-time digital self. . . . They live a high-stakes lifestyle that at any moment is subject to exposure by one sleep-deprived, thoughtless Instagram post. . . . It can result in lasting social embarrassment—a fear greater than color-coded threat levels.

Millennials experience fear of a lack of privacy. Fear of living in a fishbowl where all can see all the time. Fear of physical safety.

---

[1] The who? We're talkin' 'bout my generation. Probably, most of my generation doesn't get this footnote. The irony.

Fear of lack of popularity. Fear of a single mistake that will haunt them forever. Fear of being perfect. Fear of meeting real expectations. Fear of meeting perceived expectations. Fear of unpayable obligations. Fear of being disconnected. Fear of being left behind. Fear of showing the outside world what's true in the inside self. Fear of embarrassment, not just for a single moment in time in front of a single group of people, but recorded to be seen at any time and by any one. And this is but one generation living in today's world.

Your Fear Mosaic

Take a moment and think about what fears have been gripping, clenching, and paralyzing your heart and mind.

Will I ever climb out of this pit of financial debt?

Can I get a good-enough score on this test that my career depends on?

How much longer can my marriage be held together by a single thread?

Will my child turn from her ways and make better life decisions?

Will my wife and I ever be able to have a child?

What happens if the stock market crashes—again?

How do I move forward from my past mistakes?

What will my friends and coworkers think of me when I talk about Jesus?

Is the next round of layoffs finally going to hit me?

How do I tell my wife what I've done when it will crush her spirit?

Did we make a mistake moving to take a new job?

How am I supposed to cope with this medical diagnosis?

How do I break free from the chains of addiction?

How will my sister in Christ react when I try to biblically counsel her toward repentance?

Am I out of God's will for my life?

Does my life even matter?

Am I making a difference?

Will I ever be happy?

Why can't I just find peace in this world?

Why am I here?

What's the purpose for my life?

What happens after I die?

These questions are just a tip of the iceberg of the gigantic frozen rocks that seem to continually crush us. And each fear is personal to you and to me. While we may share some fears with others, we each have our own unique mosaic of earthly fears that paint the landscape in which we live. The first step toward living in a world full of fears is to admit that we, more often than not, live fearfully in a fear-full world. As we saw together in chapter 1, fear is a result of the Fall. We all experience it, and it's ultimately healthier if we address our fears rather than keeping them bottled up inside.

This section is intentionally short for a reason. I want you to jump ahead to this chapter's first two *James 1:22 Challenges*. For your convenience, they follow:

1. Paint your fear mosaic by listing out everything on your heart and mind that scares you.

2. Recognize that, on this side of eternity, we all experience fear. Ask God to strengthen your faith to overcome your fears in this world.

Severe Thunderstorm Warning

Have you ever been watching your favorite television show on a network station and, just at the most climactic point—whether it's the last second of the ball game, the last rose being given away, the last weigh in, the last stunt to determine the winner, the scene that will culminate years of drama—the network breaks away to the local news team for a special report because of threatening storms in the area?

In Mark's fast-moving account of Jesus and His disciples' three-year ministry, one of the most famous acts of Jesus' power is Jesus calming a severe storm that came upon them while out to sea. While many commentaries on this rightfully focus on Jesus' authority over nature, I want us to look at it from a different perspective. In these seven action-packed verses, we see the disciples fearing for their lives and doing their best Jim Cantore[2] impersonation trying to brave the elements of a devastating storm. Let's pick up the narrative in Mark 4:35:

> As evening came, Jesus said to his disciples,
> "Let's cross to the other side of the lake." [36] So they
> took Jesus in the boat and started out, leaving the

---

[2] The weatherman famous for reporting live on television in the midst of extreme weather. You always know he's not there for a sunny day of tranquility but for a hurricane, blizzard, tornado, or some other crazy weather coming your way. He's like the John the Baptist of bad weather.

crowds behind (although other boats followed). [37] But soon a fierce storm came up. High waves were breaking into the boat, and it began to fill with water.

[38] Jesus was sleeping at the back of the boat with his head on a cushion. The disciples woke him up, shouting, "Teacher, don't you care that we're going to drown?"

[39] When Jesus woke up, he rebuked the wind and said to the waves, "Silence! Be still!" Suddenly the wind stopped, and there was a great calm. [40] Then he asked them, "Why are you afraid? Do you still have no faith?"

[41] The disciples were absolutely terrified. "Who is this man?" they asked each other. "Even the wind and waves obey him!" (Mark 4:35–41)

This passage encourages us in so many ways. First, we see that we all will be in situations that will naturally cause us to fear. And that's okay. The disciples' boat is filling with water. Who knows, perhaps just one more minute of the downpour or one more powerful wave and the boat would have capsized and killed them.

Second, we see that when they are fearful, the disciples go to the one place we as Christians are called to go—to Jesus. Any fears outside of the fear of the Lord lead us to Him for safety and refuge. We are to go to Jesus even if we wonder if He really cares. Look at the disciples' question: "Teacher, don't you care that we're going to drown?" In the middle of a storm, they feel abandoned and are literally shouting to Jesus. Despite Jesus *appearing* aloof, the disciples still came to Him. In the middle of life's darkest storms, when it *appears* God doesn't care about you and your circumstance, do you still go to Him?

Let's go even deeper. After Jesus calms the storm with His voice, demonstrating His dominion over creation, look at the root of His question to the disciples. He doesn't ask only about their fear. Instead, he asks about their faith. Unhealthy fear outside of the fear of the Lord is a lapse in our faith in Him. Healthy faith in God opposes fears of anything or anyone that is not Him. If you take nothing else away from this class, please remember: *A lack of faith in God causes us to fear anything outside the healthy fear of Him.*

Continuing, do you notice what happens after Jesus acts? The disciples still fear, but the object of their fear changes, as they now fear Jesus—the biblical kind of fear. Unhealthy fear becomes healthy fear!

From Storms to Spirits

After Jesus displays His power over the natural realm, He and His disciples arrive safely from Galilee to the other side of the lake.[3] It's there we see Jesus display His power over the spiritual realm:

> So they arrived at the other side of the lake, in the region of the Gerasenes. [2] When Jesus climbed out of the boat, a man possessed by an evil spirit came out from the tombs to meet him. [3] This man lived in the burial caves and could no longer be restrained, even with a chain. [4] Whenever he was

---

[3] A serious footnote without going down a major rabbit trail: The incident we are about to witness is recorded in Matthew 8:28–34; Mark 5:1–20; and Luke 8:26–39. Some biblical readers and scholars become so confused and argumentative over supposed discrepancies to the point that biblical opponents try and use it to discredit the Bible. J. A. Martin clarifies any misconceptions in the *The Bible Knowledge Commentary: An Exposition of the Scriptures,* where he commentates on Luke 8:26: "Whereas Matthew wrote that Jesus met two demon-possessed men (Matt. 8:28–34), Luke [and Mark] wrote about only one of the two. There is some confusion as to the place where the miracle occurred. What is meant by the region of the Gerasenes? Apparently the area was named for the small town Gersa (now the ruins of Khersa) on the eastern shore, across the lake from Galilee. Matthew mentioned "the region of the Gadarenes" (Matt. 8:28), which was named for the town Gadara, about six miles southeast of the lower tip of the Sea of Galilee. Perhaps the territory around Gersa belonged to the city of Gadara (cf. comments on Mark 5:1)."

put into chains and shackles—as he often was—he
snapped the chains from his wrists and smashed
the shackles. No one was strong enough to subdue
him. [5] Day and night he wandered among the
burial caves and in the hills, howling and cutting
himself with sharp stones. (Mark 5:1–5)

The disciples, very likely still trying to process the drama of
the sail over, now get another dose. Imagine their dismay when
the welcoming party ashore is a crazed, demon-possessed maniac
who makes his home among the dead in caves with a reputation of
wrenching free from restraints multiple times. Quite different than
today's chauffer standing at the exit gate of an airport holding a
sign with your name on it, to say the least. Look, though, at Jesus'
response as the man comes *running*. Jesus isn't afraid. Jesus knows
He has dominion over the evil spirits controlling the man.

When Jesus was still some distance away, the man
saw him, ran to meet him, and bowed low before
him. [7] With a shriek, he screamed, "Why are you
interfering with me, Jesus, Son of the Most High
God? In the name of God, I beg you, don't torture me!" [8] For Jesus had already said to the spirit,
"Come out of the man, you evil spirit."

[9] Then Jesus demanded, "What is your name?"

And he replied, "My name is Legion, because
there are many of us inside this man." [10] Then the
evil spirits begged him again and again not to send
them to some distant place.

[11] There happened to be a large herd of pigs
feeding on the hillside nearby. [12] "Send us into
those pigs," the spirits begged. "Let us enter
them." (Mark 5:6–11)

I find it interesting that throughout Jesus' and then His apostles' ministries how demons and evil spirits recognize the truth of who Jesus is both in identity and power. They didn't deny Jesus' deity or power. What does that say of people today whose hearts are hardened to the point they can't even see Jesus for who He is, yet demons do?

> So Jesus gave them permission. The evil spirits came out of the man and entered the pigs, and the entire herd of about 2,000 pigs plunged down the steep hillside into the lake and drowned in the water.
>
> [14] The herdsmen fled to the nearby town and the surrounding countryside, spreading the news as they ran. People rushed out to see what had happened. [15] A crowd soon gathered around Jesus, and they saw the man who had been possessed by the legion of demons. He was sitting there fully clothed and perfectly sane, and they were all afraid. [16] Then those who had seen what happened told the others about the demon-possessed man and the pigs. [17] And the crowd began pleading with Jesus to go away and leave them alone. (Mark 5:13–17)

You'd think the crowd would be thankful for a life rescued and greater peace in the region. What about being in awe of what happened? No awe-struck, biblical fear of Jesus? Nope. Perhaps it was fear of further economic losses (2,000 pigs aren't cheap, you know), or perhaps it was fear of what Jesus would see in them. Nonetheless, they just want Jesus out of their lives.

> As Jesus was getting into the boat, the man who had been demon possessed begged to go with him. [19] But Jesus said, "No, go home to your family, and tell them everything the Lord has done for you and how merciful he has been." [20] So the man

started off to visit the Ten Towns of that region
and began to proclaim the great things Jesus had
done for him; and everyone was amazed at what
he told them. (Mark 5:18–20)

Eyewitness accounts and the reports of the townspeople (who
were mostly Gentiles—you'll see why this matters in a minute)
don't give this event its justice for us to properly comprehend what
actually happens, let alone what it means.

Bible scholar J. D. Grassmick describes the demoniac's condition: "He lived in the tombs (an outcast); he was uncontrollable
for no one could . . . subdue . . . him, not even with fetters for his
feet or a chain for his hands. He went about night and day shrieking
wildly and cutting himself with sharp stones, perhaps in a demonic
form of worship. Such behavior shows that demon possession is
not mere sickness or insanity but a desperate satanic attempt to
distort and destroy God's image in man."

This is a man so possessed by evil spirits that no humans can
control him, a man so possessed by evil spirits that no pain can stop
him from cutting himself. Like a wild animal, he can't be tamed.
The shrieking. The howling. In and out of caves. Up and down
the hills. Can you imagine living in this region? Fear grips you as
you wonder where he'll wander, being constantly reminded of the
terror as you see the broken shackles and bloody rocks during the
day and hear piercing howling throughout the night.

I think a fair contemporary comparison would be 6,000 of
the most brutally natured, savage men banding together in a town
without capable law enforcement to control them. And we live
there. We don't have a choice to move. We're there with them.
Wouldn't that scare you . . . a lot? I know I would be.

Strangely enough, perhaps even before the boat carrying Jesus
docks, the town terrorizer becomes terrorized himself. He then
bows in homage—not worship—to Jesus as he recognizes who
Jesus is—the Son of the Most High God.[4] J. D. Grassmick provides

---

[4]   Another serious footnote: Just believing that Jesus exists and is the Son of
      God doesn't save you from your sins. James, in verse 2:19, writes: "You say
      you have faith, for you believe that there is one God. Good for you! Even the

further insight: "Many evil powers controlled this man and subjected him to intense oppression. They tormented him as one combined force under the leadership of one demon, their spokesman. This accounts for the alternating singular ('my') and plural ('we') pronouns. Repeatedly the leading demon begged Jesus earnestly not to send them out of the area . . . into a lonely exile where they could not torment people. The Latin word 'Legion' . . . suggested great strength and oppression."

With J. D. Grassmick's commentary in mind, note how the demon-possessed man appeals to the One True Authority—in the name of God—for Jesus not to torture him. In other words, he is asking Jesus to show them (literally an army of evil spirits) mercy by allowing them to embody something—anything—until the final judgment at the end of the age. *Even in His earthly dealings with demons, Jesus shows mercy.* He exorcises them from the man, sending them into thousands of pigs. Immediately, the pigs swarm like bees to their nest, committing mass suicide into a nearby lake.

At this point, do you notice that the report of the exorcism focuses more on the pigs than the man? I mean, as the pigs die, the man is saved. The inspired words of this historical account focus on this for a reason. In this Gentile region (remember earlier when I said it'd be important?), herdsmen and businessmen raised pigs to sell to make their living.

Can you imagine witnessing this exorcism? Then, can you imagine watching all the assets you own to provide for you and your family being destroyed? The herdsmen literally flee—running in fear—telling anyone who would listen what happened. Receiving varying looks of shock and disbelief, the herdsmen and their passionate reporting stir a crowd to see for themselves the scene of a perceived crime—and not of the true miracle it is.

And what do they see? Jesus and a saved, transformed man. A Savior and a new creation. No longer wild, but calm. No longer self-mutilating, but self-controlled. No longer terrorized by a spiritual storm of deadly proportions, but calm as a lake's water on a

---

demons believe this, and they tremble in terror." Saving faith is *personally accepting* the free gift of eternal life offered by God through Jesus Christ's death, burial, and resurrection as payment for your sins.

sunny day. The townspeople's reaction may surprise you. They can't believe the pigs all ran into the lake and killed themselves! They aren't concerned about a single human being's spirit being saved; instead, their concern centers on multiple human beings' business losses.[5] They plead with Jesus to leave the area for fear of further economic losses. They miss the miracle. They miss the Savior.

Contrasted to the townspeople, the transformed, thankful, freed man begs with even more passion to follow Jesus. He models our response to Jesus touching our lives. Interestingly, Jesus tells the man to tell of the Lord's greet deeds and mercy. When performing miracles among the Jewish community, Jesus often tells those transformed and healed not to share what He had done, but because this formerly demon-possessed man is a Gentile in a region where Jesus (as a Jew) is not welcome, Jesus tells him to spread the word. Therefore, this maniacal menace of a non-Jewish society becomes the first grace-filled missionary to the Gentile world for Jesus Christ! And, what's the reaction to this now-sane man on a mission when he tells his story around the region? They are amazed and astonished. Or—in other words—they have a healthy fear of the Lord.

An Unhealthy Fear of the Lord

We all fear. Followers of Jesus and those who do not follow Him both fear. The only difference is that amidst commonly held fears we all share, followers of Jesus have a healthy, biblical fear of God that the latter group doesn't. Remember from our previous language lesson that we all, by nature, are sinners who deserve death. In some way, all humans fear death and what will happen after death. Christians know that only through Jesus we are saved from eternal separation from God in a literal place called Hell. Recognizing this prompts the unique, healthy fear of the Lord experienced only by followers of Jesus.

---

[5]   That attitude plays out today, over 2,000 years later. How often are people's lives hurt and lost at the expense of business and money?

The beliefs held by those who do not follow Jesus Christ vary. Some believe there is an afterlife, while others think there isn't. Of those that do believe in an afterlife, many ascribe to the popular belief system known as "karma." These individuals think that the moral merit of a person's actions in his current life, when totaled, will determine the quality of his next life. While disturbing and crude, Kurt Cobain, the late lead singer of the 1990s rock band Nirvana, illustrates this by saying, "If you're really a mean person, you're going to come back as a fly and eat poop."

Believing in karma is but one of many unhealthy spiritual beliefs. Some, if they even believe in the existence of God in the first place, see Him as a cosmic killjoy, wanting to inhibit their hedonistic desire of pleasure while living in this world. Others see God detached from this world without a care for humanity, which means that nothing on earth, including themselves, matters. Many groups worship false gods. Some may be reaching for God but fear that He cannot and will not love them because the "baggage" of their life somehow disqualifies them from His love. Others try to convince themselves that God is love and there are no moral absolutes, arguing that God will still love people regardless of what they do. Do you know anyone, including yourself, who fits in these categories?

If we are physically unhealthy, we die. If we are spiritually unhealthy, we die—for eternity. Each of these unhealthy, false fears of God, which is what each belief system is at its root, eclipses the healthy, true love of God. Unhealthy spiritual fear causes people to stumble away from the health of God's love.

Why even have this discussion? Since the beginning of recorded history, each culture has held beliefs about the afterlife. This confirms that eternity is indeed planted in every human heart, as King Solomon writes in Ecclesiastes 3:11 (ESV): "He has made everything beautiful in its time. Also, he has put eternity into man's heart, yet so that he cannot find out what God has done from the beginning to the end."

In his book entitled *When People are Big and God is Small,* Dr. Edward T. Welch succinctly summarizes this idea. While he tackles the subject of fear from more of a Christian counseling

79

point-of-view than this book, Dr. Welch posits that the fear of the Lord ranges on a spectrum of attitudes and response. On one end of the spectrum is *threat-fear*, which describes everyone, either in this life or on the coming Judgment Day, recognizing the shame of our sin standing before a holy God who is completely justified in punishing us for our sins. At this end of the spectrum, this type of fear "shrinks back from God." On the opposite end of the spectrum from *threat-fear* is the fear only followers of Jesus experience. It's the healthy fear of God we discussed earlier that encompasses reverent submission, trust, and hope. Dr. Welch calls it *worship-fear*. At both ends of the spectrum, people see their sin and God's holiness and justice. But Christians at the *worship-fear* end of the spectrum see God's grace, mercy, and love at increasing levels as this fear "draws [them] closer to God." Dr. Welch calls this *worship-fear* the "pinnacle of our response to God."

Remember our four-fold definition of fearing the Lord? While Dr. Welch uses different language, the concept and process of fearing God is the same:

1. Seeing who we are.
2. Seeing who God is.
3. Believing what God has done, is doing, and will do.
4. Responding in obedience to God.

As followers of Jesus, we are called to be reconciled reconcilers, to be used by the Holy Spirit to spread an eternal, heavenly truth in a temporal world filled with spiritual falsities. Jesus gave us the command to make disciples, which means being used by the Holy Spirit to help treat people's natural, but unhealthy, fear of the Lord along the spectrum to the healthy fear of the Lord. Unhealthy fear will no longer cause people to stumble. They'll become spiritually healthy for eternity.

Your James 1:22 Challenge

James writes to us, "But don't just listen to God's word. You must do what it says. Otherwise, you are only fooling yourselves."

Use the following five prompts to apply lessons learned from this chapter centered on God's Word to transform your life.

1. Paint your fear mosaic by writing a list of everything on your heart and mind that scares you.

2. Recognize that, on this side of eternity, we all experience fear. Ask God to strengthen your faith to overcome your fears in this world.

3. Think about the spectrum of fear described at the end of this chapter. Where are you? Are you closer to *threat-fear* or *worship-fear*? How can you move closer to the *worship-fear* end of the spectrum? At God's prompting, write down some specific actions you can take.

4. Prayerfully ask for your faith in Jesus to be strengthened by the Holy Spirit.

5. Think of one person you know who is on the *threat-fear* side of the spectrum and has yet to be drawn to a saving faith in Jesus Christ. Ask God to embolden you through the Holy Spirit to share God's eternal cure to their spiritual death.

Chapter 5:
Biology 101: Dissecting Spiritual Grasshoppers

"Look deep into nature, and then you will understand everything better."
- Albert Einstein, German-born theoretical physicist

"The LORD merely spoke, and the heavens were created. He breathed the word, and all the stars were born. He assigned the sea its boundaries and locked the oceans in vast reservoirs. Let the whole world fear the LORD, and let everyone stand in awe of him."
- The psalmist's lyrics, Psalm 33:6–8

Have you ever seen a grasshopper? Maybe you're a nature buff and have been around them since you were a kid. When I was a kid, I ran from them.[1] Now, while class is in session, I want you to stop reading and find a close-up picture of a grasshopper. Maybe you've still got some Encyclopedia Britannicas on the bookshelf, or how about that Microsoft Encarta CD that you thought was amazing while using a dial-up modem and Windows 95? I know, I know, you're more likely asking your personal digital assistant to pull pictures up for you.

Look closely at the grasshopper. I can feel the range of reactions for this insect that is famous for its role on the television show *Fear Factor*, where contestants had to eat them. Personally,

---
[1]   I still do. Like a kid.

that's when I'd change the channel. Some, like me, are probably grimacing a little bit—or a lot. Others probably think grasshoppers look pretty cool. It took me awhile to get to this point, but others may share my awe of God's creation—the detail, the intricacy of its design, the fact that it has a purpose in all of God's creation. It's really amazing to think about. In a sense, looking at a picture of a grasshopper inspires me to fear God more.

Keep this grasshopper in the back of your mind as we cover the historical record of the Israelite's journey from being slaves in Egypt to inhabiting the land promised to them by God that is recorded in Numbers chapters 13 and 14.

Fearing Man versus Fearing God

Ultimately, as we trek through our time together in biology class, we will be dissecting spiritual grasshoppers to see that our spirit fears two things: God and man. And, as we fear one more, we fear the other less. There is an inverse relationship between them. If you fear God more, you fear man less. If you fear man more, you fear God less. James writes to the early church and to us, "Come close to God, and God will come close to you. Wash your hands, you sinners; purify your hearts, for your loyalty is divided between God and the world."[2]

We understand what fearing the Lord is, but we have yet to define fearing man. Put simply, we fear man any time we are not awestruck and reverently fearing God. Let's begin the dissection following Jesus as He picks up His scalpel—His sword, also known as His Word.[3] Watch and listen to the incision as Jesus directs His disciples and, ultimately, us:

> "Look, I am sending you out as sheep among
> wolves. So be as shrewd as snakes and harmless as

---

[2] James 4:8

[3] Hebrews 4:12 (ESV): For the word of God is living and active, sharper than any two-edged sword, piercing to the division of soul and of spirit, of joints and of marrow, and discerning the thoughts and intentions of the heart.

doves. [17] But beware! For you will be handed over to the courts and will be flogged with whips in the synagogues. [18] You will stand trial before governors and kings because you are my followers. But this will be your opportunity to tell the rulers and other unbelievers about me. [19] When you are arrested, don't worry about how to respond or what to say. God will give you the right words at the right time. [20] For it is not you who will be speaking—it will be the Spirit of your Father speaking through you.

[21] "A brother will betray his brother to death, a father will betray his own child, and children will rebel against their parents and cause them to be killed. [22] And all nations will hate you because you are my followers. But everyone who endures to the end will be saved. [23] When you are persecuted in one town, flee to the next. I tell you the truth, the Son of Man will return before you have reached all the towns of Israel.

[24] "Students are not greater than their teacher, and slaves are not greater than their master. [25] Students are to be like their teacher, and slaves are to be like their master. And since I, the master of the household, have been called the prince of demons, the members of my household will be called by even worse names!

[26] "But don't be afraid of those who threaten you. For the time is coming when everything that is covered will be revealed, and all that is secret will be made known to all. [27] What I tell you now in the darkness, shout abroad when daybreak comes. What I whisper in your ear, shout from the housetops for all to hear!

[28] "Don't be afraid of those who want to kill your body; they cannot touch your soul. Fear only God, who can destroy both soul and body in hell. [29] What is the price of two sparrows—one copper coin? But not a single sparrow can fall to the ground without your Father knowing it. [30] And the very hairs on your head are all numbered. [31] So don't be afraid; you are more valuable to God than a whole flock of sparrows.

[32] "Everyone who acknowledges me publicly here on earth, I will also acknowledge before my Father in heaven. [33] But everyone who denies me here on earth, I will also deny before my Father in heaven.

[34] "Don't imagine that I came to bring peace to the earth! I came not to bring peace, but a sword." (Matthew 10:16–34)

Jesus sends His followers into the world, but not to be of it. And, it's clear we have a choice of whom we can be afraid or fear. We'll expand on these ideas in subsequent sections of this biology class. Before we do, hear again God's Word and let it penetrate your heart:

"But don't be afraid of those who threaten you. For the time is coming when everything that is covered will be revealed, and all that is secret will be made known to all. [27] What I tell you now in the darkness, shout abroad when daybreak comes. What I whisper in your ear, shout from the house-tops for all to hear!

[28] "Don't be afraid of those who want to kill your body; they cannot touch your soul. Fear only God, who can destroy both soul and body in hell. [29]

What is the price of two sparrows—one copper
coin? But not a single sparrow can fall to the
ground without your Father knowing it. [30] And
the very hairs on your head are all numbered. [31] So
don't be afraid; you are more valuable to God than
a whole flock of sparrows." (Matthew 10:26–31)

*"Don't be afraid of those who want to kill your body; they cannot
touch your soul. Fear only God, who can destroy both soul and
body in hell."* It can be no clearer than verse 28: Jesus commands
us to fear God alone because, unlike man, He can destroy our soul
in addition to our physical bodies. Man can only harm and kill our
physical, temporal bodies. God, an eternal being, has control of
our spiritual, eternal souls. For those who do not follow Jesus or,
in Jesus' words, "deny Him," this should inspire a dreadful sense
of the *threat-fear* used by Dr. Welch in our last class.

On the other hand, this same statement in verse 28 should be of
comfort for those who follow Jesus and publically proclaim God's
glory as revealed through His Son, Jesus Christ. Why? Because
God knows us so intimately, as we've previously learned. He
knows the numbers of hairs on our head and, in His character,
values us so much that He sent Jesus to die for our sins. James
writes, "He chose to give birth to us by giving us his true word. And
we, out of all creation, became his prized possession."[4] Through
Jesus, we experience a second spiritual birth that makes us God's
prized possession. Remember learning that we, the torn and tat-
tered sinful shreds of balloons, are God's masterpiece? Now we
know that God's masterpieces—followers of Jesus Christ—are His
prized possession. A masterpiece prized by God! He *delights* in
us![5] What a sense of identity! What purpose, succinctly encapsu-
lated by the Apostle Paul in 1 Thessalonians 2:4: "For we speak as
messengers approved by God to be entrusted with the Good News.

---

[4]   James 1:18

[5]   Psalm 147:11 (ESV): but the LORD takes pleasure [also translated "delights"]
      in those who fear him, in those who hope in his steadfast love.

Our purpose is to please God, not people. He alone examines the motives of our hearts."

God Sends His Followers into the World

After discussing the Spanish-American War over dinner with his family, Elbert Hubbard spent the next hour drafting an essay that would ultimately be printed over 40 million times and adapted into two movies and a radio program. Originally printed in Hubbard's magazine in February 1899, *A Message to Garcia* describes President McKinley—in the midst of escalating tensions leading up to the Spanish-American War—desiring to communicate with an insurgent leader in Cuba, which was under Spanish rule, named General Calixto Garcia. McKinley knows Garcia's forces could prove to be a valuable ally. There's only one problem: No one knows where Garcia is. He is unreachable by any means of communication; his whereabouts in Cuba unknown.

McKinley turns to Colonel Arthur L. Wagner, asking who should be sent to deliver his—the president's—message to Garcia. Being chosen by Wagner, Lieutenant Andrew Rowan, as Hubbard writes, "is given a letter to be delivered to Garcia. How 'the fellow by name of Rowan' took the letter, sealed it up in an oil-skin pouch, strapped it over his heart, in four days landed by night off the coast of Cuba from an open boat, disappeared into the jungle, and in three weeks came out on the other side of the island, having traversed a hostile country on foot, and having delivered his letter to Garcia, are things I have no special desire now to tell in detail." Rowan develops a rapport with Garcia, and Garcia's insurgents help the Americans fight against Spain on Cuban territory. Upon returning, Rowan receives the Distinguished Service Cross.

Hubbard's main point in writing *A Message to Garcia* is to show that Rowan does not ask any questions; he simply follows his commander's orders and figures out how to accomplish the mission. Concluding the essay, Hubbard writes:

> My heart goes out to the man who does his work
> when the "boss" is away, as well as when he is
> home. And the man who, when given a letter for
> Garcia, quietly takes the missive, without asking
> any idiotic questions, and with no lurking inten-
> tion of chucking it into the nearest sewer, or of
> doing aught else but deliver it, never gets "laid
> off," nor has to go on strike for higher wages.
> Civilization is one long anxious search for just
> such individuals. Anything such a man asks will
> be granted; his kind is so rare that no employer
> can afford to let him go. He is wanted in every city,
> town, and village—in every office, shop, store and
> factory. The world cries out for such; he is needed,
> and needed badly—the man who can carry a mes-
> sage to Garcia.

Business and military leaders across the world continue to use *A Message to Garcia* to inspire their own to be like Andrew Rowan—accepting a mission without complaining and accomplishing it by figuring out how best to do it on their own.

If only the Israelite scouts sent by Moses to explore the land promised to them by God could have collectively been like Lieutenant Rowan. Join me in the historical moment as recorded in Numbers 13:

> The LORD now said to Moses, [2] "Send out men to
> explore the land of Canaan, the land I am giving
> to the Israelites. Send one leader from each of the
> twelve ancestral tribes." [3] So Moses did as the
> LORD commanded him. He sent out twelve men,
> all tribal leaders of Israel, from their camp in the
> wilderness of Paran. [4] These were the tribes and
> the names of their leaders:

Tribe	Leader
Reuben	Shammua son of Zaccur
[5] Simeon	Shaphat son of Hori
[6] Judah	Caleb son of Jephunneh
[7] Issachar	Igal son of Joseph
[8] Ephraim	Hoshea son of Nun
[9] Benjamin	Palti son of Raphu
[10] Zebulun	Gaddiel son of Sodi
[11] Manasseh son of Joseph	Gaddi son of Susi
[12] Dan	Ammiel son of Gemalli
[13] Asher	Sethur son of Michael
[14] Naphtali	Nahbi son of Vophsi
[15] Gad	Geuel son of Maki

> [16] These are the names of the men Moses sent out to explore the land. (Moses called Hoshea son of Nun by the name Joshua.) (Numbers 13:1–16)

Each of Israel's twelve tribes has a leader representing them as part of a group of spies who are to travel through the Promised Land. Pay special attention to the men named in verses 6 and 8, the leaders of Judah and Ephraim, respectively. Moses selects Caleb, who is the son of Jephunneh, to represent the tribe of Judah. Moses then picks Hoshea, the son of Nun, to represent the tribe of Ephraim. You likely know Hoshea by his more familiar name: Joshua (see verse 16).

As the group of twelve sets out on their spy mission commissioned by God through Moses to check out the Promised Land for Israel, focus on Caleb and Joshua. They differ from their peers by sharing the characteristics of Lieutenant Rowan when delivering President McKinley's message to General Garcia. Additionally, I think it's noteworthy that, as God the Father sends the twelve scouts into their Promised Land, over 1,000 years later God the

Son, Jesus, sends His twelve disciples into their world, just as Jesus commands all of His followers to go throughout our world today. This begs the question for us: *Are we going into the world, sharing Jesus' message like Rowan taking the president's message to Garcia?*

God Commands His Followers to Be in the World, but Not of the World

Early in my professional career, I had the privilege to serve in my home state's government. The office where I worked oversaw more than fifteen varied divisions and agencies, one of which was the Purchasing Division. Not unlike other federal, state, and local governments, previous civil servants of the 20th century abused their power to pad the pockets of friends, family, and themselves by procuring needed (and unneeded) goods and services "for government use." Upon such discoveries, the next generation of politicians and bureaucrats rightly and nobly enacted stringent laws, rules, and regulations to prevent public procurement from such corruption.

Perhaps calling the state's procurement process at the time I served "cumbersome" because of all these laws, rules, and regulations is an understatement. As a result of the overly complicated system, state taxpayers of the 21st century ended up having to pay more for goods and services simply because a vendor forgot to put one piece of paper in one of the two identical bid packages they are required to submit. Did the missing piece of paper have a material impact on the prospective provider's goods or services? Not in the least. However, because an antiquated rule required both bid packages to be identical and include all required documents, the bid—regardless if it was the lowest bid by tens or hundreds of thousands of dollars—has to be disqualified as the law stipulates.[6]

One could easily argue the pendulum had swung too far the other way. However, this illustrates the importance of following directions—whether they are spelled out in purchasing rules or

---

[6] Just in case you were wondering, purchasing reform subsequently enacted removed that particular archaic rule.

given by Israel's chosen leader on the way to the Promised Land. Moses' specific instructions for the group of twelve scouts are outlined in Numbers 13:17–24. As we read and listen with our eyes, I want you to consider what is *not* included in these instructions:

> Moses gave the men these instructions as he sent them out to explore the land: "Go north through the Negev into the hill country. [18] See what the land is like, and find out whether the people living there are strong or weak, few or many. [19] See what kind of land they live in. Is it good or bad? Do their towns have walls, or are they unprotected like open camps? [20] Is the soil fertile or poor? Are there many trees? Do your best to bring back samples of the crops you see." (It happened to be the season for harvesting the first ripe grapes.)
>
> [21] So they went up and explored the land from the wilderness of Zin as far as Rehob, near Lebo-hamath. [22] Going north, they passed through the Negev and arrived at Hebron, where Ahiman, Sheshai, and Talmai—all descendants of Anak— lived. (The ancient town of Hebron was founded seven years before the Egyptian city of Zoan.) [23] When they came to the valley of Eshcol, they cut down a branch with a single cluster of grapes so large that it took two of them to carry it on a pole between them! They also brought back samples of the pomegranates and figs. [24] That place was called the valley of Eshcol (which means "cluster"), because of the cluster of grapes the Israelite men cut there. (Numbers 13:17–24)

In these verses, Moses lays out a specific path for the group of twelve to follow through the Promised Land. The magnitude of the charted course can be lost to us today because of our lack of knowledge about ancient geography. In contemporary terms, this path was approximately 500 miles long, one way. So, the group covered 1,000 miles over forty days, averaging approximately twenty-five miles a day. Walking and hiking, walking and hiking, and walking and hiking twenty-five miles per day after day after day for forty days. Humans tend to walk around three miles per hour, so this is certainly plausible, although it had to be mentally, physically, emotionally, and spiritually draining.

Think about it, though. It wasn't just walking and hiking. This was a caravan of a group of twelve. They had to describe the different cities and towns and bring back samples of fruit; it wasn't just a joyride for forty days. Often, the scene described in verse 23—two men carrying such a huge cluster of grapes because it was *that* heavy—is depicted in art, from drawings and engravings to sculptures. Two men, one walking in front of the other, struggling to hold a thick branch over their shoulders with a cluster of grapes so big it almost touches the ground hanging between them. Can you imagine a cluster of grapes that would look like that?! That's not something you're going to see at the local grocery store or supermarket chain.

So, with all this background in mind, I want to consider what is *not* included in these instructions, in the almost-1,000 mile journey, with the grapes so heavy that two people had to carry them. God, through Moses, commanded the group *not* to settle in the land or become like those living throughout the Promised Land. In verses 17–24 of this inspired historical account, we see that God commands His followers to be in the world, but not of the world. God didn't tell the group of twelve to adopt the customs of those living in the land or to adopt the various religions of the groups settled there. In other words, the new environment these men are to be subjected to is not to harm their relationship with God. Despite their surroundings, they are to remain faithful to the mission God gave them.

Does this sound familiar? It's repeated throughout the Old and New Testaments. Specifically, think about Jesus' words recorded in John 15:19 when He is talking to His disciples about the world and what they, as His followers, will face: "The world would love you as one of its own if you belonged to it, but you are no longer part of the world. I chose you to come out of the world, so it hates you." Jesus' words apply to us, too. Just like the His disciples—and just like this group of twelve scouts—we are not to let the ungodly, evil principles and practices of the world negatively affect our relationship with God.

God Gives Us a Choice of Whom to Fear

Have you ever felt like you just don't belong? A place most of us felt this way was in middle and high school. We've all felt it one time or another while moving to a new town, walking into a new job, or going on a blind date. We have felt it while sharing our faith with our group of friends who don't go to church, and living in a world falling further and further away from God's original, perfect design.

The Israelite caravan of scouts sure feels that way. We'll see that those who are already inhabiting the Promised Land don't care or think too much of them, just like the world hated Jesus' disciples and apostles, and just like the world today doesn't care much for what—or who—we as Christians center our lives on. This reinforces the fact that we are caught in a spiritual battle between God and Satan, the prince of this world. We have a choice. God allows His followers to choose whether to fear Him or fear man. We see this choice as we pick up the narrative:

> After exploring the land for forty days, the men returned [26] to Moses, Aaron, and the whole community of Israel at Kadesh in the wilderness of Paran. They reported to the whole community what they had seen and showed them the fruit they had taken from the land. [27] This was their report to Moses: "We entered the land you sent us to explore, and it is indeed a bountiful country—a land flowing with milk and honey. Here is the kind of fruit it produces. [28] But the people living there are powerful, and their towns are large and fortified. We even saw giants there, the descendants

of Anak! [29] The Amalekites live in the Negev, and the Hittites, Jebusites, and Amorites live in the hill country. The Canaanites live along the coast of the Mediterranean Sea and along the Jordan Valley."

[30] But Caleb tried to quiet the people as they stood before Moses. "Let's go at once to take the land," he said. "We can certainly conquer it!"

[31] But the other men who had explored the land with him disagreed. "We can't go up against them! They are stronger than we are!" [32] So they spread this bad report about the land among the Israelites: "The land we traveled through and explored will devour anyone who goes to live there. All the people we saw were huge. [33] We even saw giants there, the descendants of Anak. Next to them we felt like grasshoppers, and that's what they thought, too!" (Numbers 13:25–33)

The leader-scouts' report describes the land just as God promised—a land flowing with milk and honey. Can you picture the two men presenting the gigantic cluster of grapes to Moses and Aaron in front of all the Israelites? Do you notice how the group starts out with a positive report, affirming God's promises about the land He is giving to the Israelites? However, optimism and hope are suddenly thrown out the window when the leader-scouts describe the land's inhabitants.

Despite Caleb's plea of faithfulness in God's covenant promise and protection, the majority of Israel's leaders don't stop there. They drop the "grasshopper bomb" on the nation of Israel. Grasshoppers. *Really?* The vast majority of the group of twelve feel like grasshoppers. Remember the picture you saw earlier? That's what ten leaders of God's chosen people feel like. Instead of seeing their Giant, Truly Larger-than-Life God, they see themselves as teeny, tiny, weak grasshoppers. They miss the true promises of the Creator because of their false perceptions of His creation.

Have you ever felt like a grasshopper? When you're looking at everything in the world around you except toward the God who loves you and goes before you? I've sure felt like it, sitting alone on my cold bathroom floor thinking about anything and everything except God's faithfulness and love for me. I saw all my thoughts swirling around me as the giant equivalent of the descendants of Anak. We'll discuss how God transforms us from a grasshopper to a giant later when we're outside the classroom and in the Lab of Life.

After hearing this report, all the Israelites jump into "grass-hopper mode" with the leader-scouts. In the opening verses of Numbers 14, they question God and conspire to choose their own leader to replace God's appointed, Moses. The Israelites are planning a coup of God's leader. Then, beginning in Numbers 14:7, the only ones faithful to God and His promises—Moses, Aaron, Caleb, and Joshua—speak to the entire camp of Israel:

> They said to all the people of Israel, "The land
> we traveled through and explored is a wonderful
> land! ⁸ And if the LORD is pleased with us, he will
> bring us safely into that land and give it to us. It is
> a rich land flowing with milk and honey. ⁹ Do not
> rebel against the LORD, and don't be afraid of the
> people of the land. They are only helpless prey to
> us! They have no protection, but the LORD is with
> us! Don't be afraid of them!" (Numbers 14:7–9)

Remember, God allows His followers to choose whether to fear Him or fear man. Together, let's focus on the faithful and their words spoken in verse nine: "Do not rebel against the LORD, and don't be afraid of the people of the land. They are only helpless prey to us! They have no protection, but the LORD is with us! Don't be afraid of them!"

I want us to see two points in this verse. First, to fear man is to directly rebel against God. Moses, Aaron, Caleb, and Joshua equate being afraid of the land's inhabitants as being rebellious against God. Look at the conjunction *and* in the first sentence of verse nine. The two ideas—directly rebelling against God and fearing man—are one and the same.

Now look at the second half of verse nine. Listen to what the faithful four say: "[All the inhabitants of the Promised Land] are only helpless prey to us! They have no protection, but the LORD is with us! Don't be afraid of them!" Contrasted to fearing man, to fear God is to respond in faith to God's promises. Moses, Aaron, Caleb, and Joshua, fearing God, know that God is faithful and will lead them to victory. Moses, Aaron, Caleb, and Joshua know that, to God, the giants the Israelites face, and the giants we face today, are smaller than grasshoppers compared to Him. However, the rest of Israelites aren't seeing it that way, and God appears to them in verse 10, basically asking, "What's it going to take for you Israelites to believe me? I've even done miracle after miracle."

The historical record from Numbers 14:12–38 details Moses pleading with God not to destroy the disobedient Israelites on the spot. Let's look quickly at an example of this exchange:

> "In keeping with your magnificent, unfailing love,
> please pardon the sins of the people, just as you
> have forgiven them ever since they left Egypt."
>
> [20] Then the LORD said, "I will pardon them as you
> have requested." (Numbers 14:19–20)

This doesn't mean God doesn't punish the Israelites, because He is just. God decrees that no Israelites except Joshua and Caleb, the two faithful scouts, will enter the Promised Land. Look at verse 30 when God gives a message to Moses and Aaron to relay to the Israelites:

> You [the Israelites] will not enter and occupy the
> land I [the LORD] swore to give you. The only
> exceptions will be Caleb son of Jephunneh and
> Joshua son of Nun. (Numbers 19:30)

God continues doling out His just punishment in verses 36 and 37, as He strikes the ten unfaithful scouts dead with a plague. Joshua and Caleb are the only two of the twelve to survive. Let's pick up the story in verse Numbers 14:39:

> When Moses reported the LORD's words to all the Israelites, the people were filled with grief. [40] Then they got up early the next morning and went to the top of the range of hills. "Let's go," they said. "We realize that we have sinned, but now we are ready to enter the land the LORD has promised us."
>
> [41] But Moses said, "Why are you now disobeying the LORD's orders to return to the wilderness? It won't work. [42] Do not go up into the land now. You will only be crushed by your enemies because the LORD is not with you. [43] When you face the Amalekites and Canaanites in battle, you will be slaughtered. The LORD will abandon you because you have abandoned the LORD."
>
> [44] But the people defiantly pushed ahead toward the hill country, even though neither Moses nor the Ark of the LORD's Covenant left the camp. [45] Then the Amalekites and the Canaanites who lived in those hills came down and attacked them and chased them back as far as Hormah. (Numbers 14:39–45)

If you're like me, you're immediately left wondering what happens between verses 39 and 40. The Israelites are filled with grief because God has justly punished them for their sins. They've just seen ten of their leaders struck dead by God. So, what do they decide to do next? They decide to disobey God *again*! God just told the Israelites that none of them would enter the Promised Land, but they decide *the very next day* that they are ready to go anyway. It's easy looking back to play "Monday Morning Quarterback" over

3,000 years later; however, I have to look at my life first. How many times have I succumbed to temptation only minutes after reading God's Word that clearly admonishes what I am doing? Too many to count—days or sometimes hours or just minutes after reading. Are you in the same huddle I am?

God Allows His Followers to Fear Him, Others, or Themselves

Feeling humbled right now? God's Word is timeless. Today, you and I are guilty of the same sins the Israelites committed millennia ago. As with the Israelites, God allows His followers to choose whether to fear Him, others, or themselves. We can either fear God, fear others, or fear ourselves.

Remember, one sense of the word *fear* in the Bible is to revere, worship, or be awestruck. When we fear ourselves, we forget who we are and upon whom we are to depend. We elevate ourselves to a level where we don't think we need to listen to God. This is a form of idolatry. Specifically, it's pride. Pride is the idolatry of self. It's the same sin that got Satan cast out of Heaven and the same sin that got Adam and Eve cast out of the Garden of Eden. It is the same sin that can wreak havoc on the intimacy of our relationship with God and with others.

Remember *The Selfie Generation*? While society limits it to a generation born between certain years, I submit to you that all of humanity—since Adam and Eve to us and those yet to be born—are card-carrying members of *The Selfie Generation—The Generation of the Self.*

Look what happens when pride characterizes us:

> But the people defiantly pushed ahead toward the hill country, even though neither Moses nor the Ark of the LORD's Covenant left the camp. [45] Then the Amalekites and the Canaanites who lived in those hills came down and attacked them and chased them back as far as Hormah. (Numbers 14:44–45)

We've all been there in our Christian walk, just like the Israelites. Stubborn. Continuously trying to pursue our own agenda when God makes it perfectly clear what we are to do. Take the following story, for example:

> A man is in his house during a flood. He begins praying to God to rescue him. He has a vision in his head of God's hand reaching down from heaven and lifting him to safety. The water starts to rise around his house and begins to flood inside. His neighbor urges him to leave, offering him a ride to safety if he simply walks out through a path still passable despite the rising waters. The man yells back, "I am waiting for God to save me." The neighbor, shaking his head, drives off in his pickup truck.
>
> The man continues to pray, holding on to his vision. As the water rises from the bottom floors of his house, he eventually climbs up onto the roof. Then, a boat motors by with some people aboard, heading for safe ground. With room left in the boat, they call to the man to grab a rope they are getting ready to throw and take him to safety. He confidently tells them that he is waiting for God to save him, motioning them to go on without him. Shaking their heads, the boat and its people speed away to safety.
>
> The man continues to pray, believing with all his heart that he will be saved by God, as the flood waters continue to rise. A helicopter flies overhead and, with the engine buzzing in the background, a voice comes over a loudspeaker offering to lower a ladder for the man to climb up to safety from his roof, which is now only a few feet from the rushing floodwaters. Waving the helicopter away, the man shouts back that he is waiting for God to save him. Like the pickup truck and the boat, the

> helicopter reluctantly leaves the man behind. Soon thereafter, the floodwaters sweep over the roof, catching and sweeping the man away. Needless to say, he drowns.
>
> When he reaches heaven, he asks, "God, why did you not save me? I believed in you with all my heart. Why did you let me drown?"
>
> God replies, "I sent you a pickup truck, a boat, and a helicopter, and you refused all of them. What else could I possibly do for you?"

While humorous and ultimately limiting God's power, this illustration clearly shows how you and I can sometimes be bullheaded and stubborn toward God because you and I are just like the Israelites in Numbers 13–14.

With the biology classroom smelling of spiritual dissection, let's review: God sends us to be in the world, but not of the world. He allows us to choose whether to fear God or man, which includes fearing others or ourselves. May we all embrace the Apostle Paul's mindset he describes in Galatians 1:10: "Obviously, I'm not trying to win the approval of people, but of God. If pleasing people were my goal, I would not be Christ's servant."

The dissection is complete. Please remember to wash your hands and heart before we head to math class.

Your James 1:22 Challenge

James writes to us, "But don't just listen to God's word. You must do what it says. Otherwise, you are only fooling yourselves." Use the following five prompts to apply lessons learned from this chapter centered on God's Word to transform your life.

1. What do you see when you look at a grasshopper? Do you see a nasty insect? Do you see the intricacies of one of God's creations? Try looking at it as God's handiwork. Even grasshoppers can inspire us to worship our Creator God.

2. Consciously think about whether you are fearing God or fearing man as you go about your day's various activities. Make a journal of the day's events—from your thoughts and attitudes to your actions—and write whether you acted more out of a fear of God or out of a fear of man. For extra credit, try doing this for a week.

3. In what areas of your life are you doing more than just living in this world? In other words, in what areas of your life are you living *of the world*? Remember, God commands His followers to live in the world, but not of it.

4. When you look in the mirror, do you see yourself as God's masterpiece? When you look at others, do you see them as God's masterpieces?

5. Ask a Christian brother or sister who will speak the truth in love to you (Bible-speak for saying something that may temporarily hurt or sting you but will help you in the long run) the following question: "Am I more like Joshua and Caleb, or am I like a spiritual grasshopper?" Work together to write down three ways you can be like Joshua and Caleb. Then, write down three areas in your life you are stubbornly holding onto, refusing to give to God. Ask God in prayer to help you let go and turn them over to Him.

Chapter 6:
Math 101: Calculating Your Spiritual Fear Factor

"Mathematics is the language with which God wrote the Universe."
- Galileo Galilei, Italian astronomer, physicist, engineer, philosopher, and mathematician

"And he [Judah's leader Amaziah] did what was right in the eyes of the LORD, yet not with a whole heart."
- The author of 2 Chronicles, 2 Chronicles 25:2 (ESV)

W e were all kids once, and I'm pretty sure we all verbalized or thought the following at least a few times in school: "Why do I need to learn this? I'm never going to use it in life." The thought pops into our mind if we don't like a particular subject or aren't performing particularly well in it. Akin to the classic parental comeback little Ralphie knew all too well in response to his pleas for an official Red Ryder, carbine action, two-hundred shot range model air rifle ("Oh no, you'll shoot your eye out!"), you and I are met with the classic parental answer of "Because you have to." My guess is that those of us who are parents parents today now play the same card we used to abhor.

The subject of mathematics reigns at the top as the subject most questioned. *X plus Y equals what? Negative b plus or minus the square root of b squared minus 4ac, all over 2a?* My eyes—and brain—just glazed over as I typed that.[1] For me, it was in my first semester of college in Calculus 2. When we started talking about how certain formulas behave approaching negative and positive infinity, I scrambled to make it to the end of the semester. When I heard Calc 3 was named as such because it started talking about math in *three* dimensions—instead of two—I ran far, far away into the liberal arts and social sciences.[2]

Questioning the relevancy of mathematics translated[3] from kid-dom and students of all ages to the pages of our nation's largest newspapers in 2012, Roger C. Schank, a cognitive scientist, artificial intelligence theorist, and education reformer, who had taught at Stanford and Yale Universities and was the John Evans Professor Emeritus of Computer Science, Psychology, and Education at Northwestern University, in addition to being the former head of the Institute for the Learning Sciences, and the author of *Teaching Minds: How Cognitive Science Can Save Our Schools*[4] wrote:

> Whenever I meet anyone who wants to talk about education, I immediately ask them to tell me the quadratic equation. Almost no one ever can.[5] . . . Yet, we all seem to believe that everyone must learn algebra. Reasoning mathematically is a nice skill but one that is not relevant to most of life. We reason about many things: parenting, marriage, careers, finances, business, politics. Do we learn how to reason about these things by learning algebra? The idea is absurd.

---

[1] Yet I am simultaneously sad and surprised I know and remember what it is.

[2] That's not the reason for Calc 3's name, but it might as well be.

[3] Used here as a math term, for the record. Look it up.

[4] Whew. That was a mouthful. To paraphrase: The dude's really smart.

[5] Guess what the formula is in the second paragraph. I'm almost a nobody! Wait . . .

Here, a really, really, really smart and brilliant man says we don't need to learn math. If you're a math student reading this book, you are now armed with a comeback to your parents. You're welcome. Unfortunately, I happen to disagree with a scholar who is much smarter than me. But, I have the power of the pen at the moment. It's like the power of the pulpit. The bully pulpit. So, I win this round as we head to math class in our journey together. *Math class is now in session.*

Simple Division and a Curmudgeon Uncle

As you hopefully know by now, the title of this book is *Spiritual Fear Factor: Living Marked by the Fear of God to Transform a World Centered on the Fear of Man.* What you may not realize, though, is how central the word *factor* is to our study. In today's class, we'll see that our "Spiritual Fear Factor" is a mathematical principle that will help us compare, at any time, how much we fear God and simultaneously how much we fear man. Our Spiritual Fear Factor enumerates the relationship in a way that makes it even easier for us to understand.

Ratios or fractions are used in mathematics to define a relationship between a portion of something to its whole, or the amount of something compared to an amount of something else. For example, if a pie is cut into eight pieces, and your curmudgeon of an uncle eats seven pieces, then only one lonely piece of pie is left. If we fractionalize this poor pie predicament, we say there is one-eighth (commonly written out as 1/8) of the pie left. We are comparing the remaining portion of pie to its original whole.

$$\frac{\text{There's only 1 piece of pie left}}{\text{Of 8 total original pieces}} = \frac{1}{8}$$

Before your eyes glaze over, and the thought of eating pie bombards your brain, or you start twitching as flashbacks from school suddenly rush to the forefront of your mind, I need you to remember the parts of a fraction. Do the words *numerator* and *denominator* ring a bell? The numerator is the top number in a fraction, and the denominator is the bottom number. So, in the aforementioned example, the number one is the numerator, and the number eight is the denominator. Shown pictorially:

$$\frac{\text{Numerator}}{\text{Denominator}}$$

Now, let's say you know ahead of time that your curmudgeon of an uncle is going to eat almost the entire pie because he does it at every holiday meal. I mean *every* meal. It's ridiculous. You've watched him do it for *decades*. Therefore, for every three ounces of fruit filling you add to the pie, you mix in one ounce of laxative. You want your uncle to reap what he sows.[6] Motives and results aside, mathematically speaking, the ratio of fruit filling to laxative is three-to-one (commonly written out as "3:1"). The ratio describes the relative amount of the two substances; in this case, fruit filling and laxatives.

$$\frac{\text{For every 3 ounces of fruit filling}}{\text{There is 1 ounce of laxative}} = \frac{3}{1} \text{ or } 3{:}1$$

Spiritual Fear Factor Defined

So, when I use the term "Spiritual Fear Factor," I am referring to the relationship or ratio between what—or whom—your spirit fears. Remember, our Spiritual Fear Factor compares how much we are fearing God and, simultaneously, fearing man at a particular point in time. Mathematically, it looks like this:

---

[6] For the record, maybe, but I want to stress that this is a hypothetical situation to illustrate a mathematical concept. I do not have an uncle who is a curmudgeon, nor do I endorse adding laxatives to pies. But, if this book happens to be your bathroom reading material, I'm chuckling right now.

Spiritual Fear Factor $= \dfrac{\text{Fear of God}}{\text{Fear of Man}}$

Think back to biology class for a moment. As part of the lesson, we dissected the fear of man into two parts: The fear of others and the fear of ourselves. To illustrate this point mathematically, using the above formula, we see our Spiritual Fear Factor can now be written as follows:

Spiritual Fear Factor $= \dfrac{\text{Fear of God}}{\text{Fear of Man}} = \dfrac{\text{Fear of God}}{(\text{Fear of Others})\,(\text{Fear of Self})}$

See the difference? We've broken down the fear of man further into its two subcomponents: The fear of others and the fear of self. Together, both comprise the fear of man.

Now, recall from biology class Jesus' words spoken as recorded in Matthew 10:28: "Don't be afraid of those who want to kill your body; they cannot touch your soul. Fear only God, who can destroy both soul and body in hell." We can fear others, we can idolize ourselves, or we can fear God. These levels of fear are constantly changing—from one life stage to the next, from year to year, month to month, day to day, hour to hour, or even minute by minute.

Keeping up so far with these foundational concepts? Let's see what happens when we start plugging some numbers into the equation.

An Increasing Spiritual Fear Factor

When our fear of God is increasing, that means the numerator is becoming larger and larger with bigger numbers. These bigger numbers signify a higher level of fearing God. At the same time our fear of God is increasing, our fear of man is decreasing. The numbers in the denominator are becoming smaller and smaller. When you divide a big number (in the numerator) by a small number (in the denominator), the result is a really big number. For example, say the numerical value of you fearing God is 50 (the numerator), and the numerical value of fearing man is 2 (the denominator). When you divide 50 by 2, your Spiritual Fear Factor is 25.

$$\frac{50\text{ (the numerator, representing your fear of God)}}{2\text{ (the denominator, representing your fear of man)}} = 25\text{ (your Spiritual Fear Factor)}$$

Now, let's say you are beginning to fear God more than you have because the Holy Spirit continues to provide you with greater insight into who you are; who God is; and what God has done, is doing, and will do; which then causes you to walk more and more by faith in obedience to God's Word empowered by His Spirit. To illustrate this, let's say your fear of God increases from 50 to 100, and your denominator decreases from 2 to 1. Shown pictorially:

$$\frac{100\text{ (the numerator, representing your fear of God)}}{1\text{ (the denominator, representing your fear of man)}} = 100\text{ (your Spiritual Fear Factor)}$$

Your Spiritual Fear Factor moves from 25 to 100. This higher number signifies the positive spiritual changes in your life. You're living with a higher Spiritual Fear Factor. Generally speaking, this positive spiritual change can be represented by the following:

$$\text{Spiritual Fear Factor} = \frac{\text{Fear of God}}{\text{(Fear of Others) (Fear of Self)}} = \frac{\uparrow}{\downarrow} = \Uparrow$$

The main takeaway? Living with an increasing Spiritual Fear Factor is a sign of spiritual growth and being conformed more into the image of Jesus.

A Decreasing Spiritual Fear Factor

The converse, or opposite, holds true, as well. If you begin to fear God less and fear man more (whether it's fearing others, yourself, or both), then the numerator will decrease while the denominator will increase. To show this, let's start by recalling the first example we used with our fear of God valued at 50 and our fear of man valued at 2, which equaled a Spiritual Fear Factor of 25:

$$\frac{50 \text{ (the numerator, representing your fear of God)}}{2 \text{ (the denominator, representing your fear of man)}} = 25 \text{ (your Spiritual Fear Factor)}$$

Let's say your spiritual walk is not as in step with God as much now. You've endured testing and temptation but are becoming weak and not turning to God for strength. Maybe you're being outright stubborn like the ancient Israelites and rebelling against God in a particular area of your life. Temptation causes you to believe the grass is greener on the other side of the fence between righteousness and sin, so you jump over the fence and let temptation give birth to sin, as James describes.[7] Although it's not used as commonly today, Christians past call this condition "backsliding."

John Rice, in his 1943 book appropriately entitled *The Backslider*, writes:

> A backslider is a [follower of Jesus Christ] who falls into sin. [Someone who does not follow Jesus Christ] cannot be a backslider. You have to go somewhere before you can slide back. . . . It may be outrageous and gross sin known to everyone, or it may be merely coldness of heart, a lukewarmness of heart instead of the burning fire of love for God. But when a Christian loses any of his joy, or loses part of his sweet fellowship with God, or

---

[7]   James 1:12–15 (ESV): Blessed is the man who remains steadfast under trial, for when he has stood the test he will receive the crown of life, which God has promised to those who love him. [13] Let no one say when he is tempted, "I am being tempted by God," for God cannot be tempted with evil, and he himself tempts no one. [14] But each person is tempted when he is lured and enticed by his own desire. [15] Then desire when it has conceived gives birth to sin, and sin when it is fully grown brings forth death.

falls into sin, then he is a backslider. . . . We have many examples of this in the Bible. . . . Noah got drunk . . . Abraham deceived . . . Moses lost his temper. . . . David, a man after God's own heart . . . committed adultery . . . and then had her husband Uriah slain to hide his sin. . . . Peter denied Christ and . . . later . . . fearing the Jewish Christians, played the coward again, and led even good Barnabas away with his dissimulations. . . . So the saints of the Bible fell into sin. They were backsliders. These examples should humble us and teach us that even the mightiest of God's saints sometimes backslide, fall into sin, and so lose the sweet joy that every Christian ought to have. A Christian who backslides is like a child who disobeys his parents. It does not affect his sonship but it affects his fellowship, his joy, and the approval of the Father.

A couple key takeaways on Christian backsliding:

1. Backsliding does not affect our eternal salvation, but it does affect our intimacy of fellowship on this side of Heaven and the rewards we will receive in Heaven.

2. Abraham and Peter are examples of those who backslid because they feared man more than they feared God. They had a decreasing Spiritual Fear Factor during certain times in their lives.[8]

3. God provides a way to restore our intimate fellowship and joy with Him, which we'll discuss in the Lab of Life later in our journey.

---

[8]   Abraham feared powerful rulers would take his wife, Sarah, to be theirs. Peter Denied Jesus and cursed himself because he feared the crowd and what they'd do to him.

Let's put some numbers with this example. If your fear of God drops from 50 to 15 while your fear of man simultaneously rises from 2 to 30, then your Spiritual Fear Factor is calculated by dividing 15 by 30, which equals 1/2 or 0.5. Written out mathematically:

$$\frac{\textbf{15}\ {\scriptstyle\text{(the numerator, representing your fear of God)}}}{\textbf{30}\ {\scriptstyle\text{(the denominator, representing your fear of man)}}} = \frac{\textbf{1}}{\textbf{2}}\ \text{or}\ \textbf{0.5}\ {\scriptstyle\text{(your Spiritual Fear Factor)}}$$

Your Spiritual Fear Factor decreases from 25 to 0.5, which numerically illustrates your backsliding.

Generally speaking, the lower number signifies the destructive spiritual changes in your life. When you fear others or yourself more than you fear God, then your fear of God is small. This means the numerator in your equation is small. Simultaneously, the denominator is big. A small number divided by a big number equals a small number. This means you're living with a lower Spiritual Fear Factor and need to repent and fear God more. This negative spiritual change can be represented by the following:

$$\textbf{Spiritual Fear Factor} = \frac{\textbf{Fear of God}}{\textbf{(Fear of Others) (Fear of Self)}} = \frac{\downarrow}{\uparrow} = \Downarrow$$

This condition is not good in biblical terms, and I have a special name for you and me when this equation characterizes us. You and I are . . .

Spiritual grasshoppers.

Do you know that certain types of grasshoppers or locusts are characterized by blending in with their environment? That's applicable to us as Christians. If we are living lives not marked by the fear of God, then we're going to look an awful lot like the world around us. Blending in. Not being the light we are called to be by God and feeling small compared to the descendants of Anak.

When you and I fear others or ourselves more than we fear God, we are spiritual grasshoppers! I don't want to be a spiritual grasshopper. I would much rather do what King Solomon concludes at the end of the book of Ecclesiastes and fear God instead. So, after learning how to calculate our Spiritual Fear Factor, live your life marked by the biblical fear of God. *Don't be a spiritual grasshopper!* Allow the Holy Spirit to convict you of sin, and then repent and walk obediently by faith. In other words: *Fear God instead.*

If you understand these concepts, then you are ready to move from the traditional classroom setting into the Lab of Life to apply these principles to our everyday walk. Music, hiking, and stone-throwing await!

Your James 1:22 Challenge

James writes to us, "But don't just listen to God's word. You must do what it says. Otherwise, you are only fooling yourselves." Use the following five prompts to apply lessons learned from this chapter centered on God's Word to transform your life.

1. Calculate your current Spiritual Fear Factor. Is the fear of God a factor for you? Are you a spiritual grasshopper?

2. Identify situations that cause your Spiritual Fear Factor to increase. Explore the reasons why.

3. Identify situations that cause your Spiritual Fear Factor to decrease. Explore the reasons why.

4. Ask God to increase your fear of Him and decrease your fear of others and yourself. Write down the ways the Holy Spirit tells you to accomplish this.

5. Learn to love math.[9]

---

[9] Just kidding!

Part 2:

Learning in the Lab of Life

Chapter 7: Musing on Music

"It's often said that a picture is worth a thousand words but the same image can have different meanings across cultures. Music, however, may bridge the cultural divide: a new study has shown that regardless of culture or previous exposure, people were accurately able to recognize three emotions in Western music—happiness, sadness, and fear."
-    Karen Sprey, author for *Gizmag*

"Make a joyful noise to the LORD, all the earth; break forth into joyous song and sing praises! Sing praises to the LORD with the lyre, with the lyre and the sound of melody! With trumpets and the sound of the horn make a joyful noise before the King, the LORD!
-    The psalmist's lyrics, Psalm 98:4–6 (ESV)

S heer silence. In today's world, it's one of the most elusive and often uncomfortable environments. From driving cars to doing classwork, we rarely want to do so without listening to *something*, whether the sounds of nature; background noise from a television, radio, computer, or phone; or even the constant, annoying, different sounds of a construction project right outside your apartment.[1] Think about it. On hold waiting to speak with technical support? Jam out to some canned hold music! Are you an introvert, traveling shoulder-to-shoulder in a crammed elevator going up to the 97th floor? Just focus on the elevator music, and it will all be over soon. Keep telling yourself that.

---

[1]   Which I'm experiencing as I write this. Argh!

We're now exiting the classroom to learn in the Lab of Life. Remember the days of piling onto a bus for a field trip? Well, it's your turn to walk up the stairs, greet the driver with a friendly smile, and pick your seat.[2] At least this is a bus that has on-board music to listen to as we drive a short distance toward our destination: the woods. Here's a fair warning: This isn't a mindless travel, though. In fact, it may be the hardest lesson of our journey together. You may think I'm way off base. You may sharply disagree with me. You may wonder why this is even a lesson in the first place.[3] All I ask is that you think about what I'm saying. Or, really, what others are singing.

It just so happens that the driver has the radio tuned to a local pop station, and we're going to listen through the lens of all we've learned. It's easy for Christians to recognize songs that explicitly do not hold to Christian values, whether its lyrics full of curse words or lyrics promoting—how should I describe them—unsavory, sinful activities. But what about songs that don't have either? It's these "safe" secular songs that can subtly affect our Spiritual Fear Factor without us even realizing it.[4]

Happy

Sometimes, I tune into NBC's *The Voice*. Compared to other find-the-next-music-star-next-door shows, I've always been struck by the quality of singers but, more importantly, how positive and helpful the show's celebrity coaches are toward the participants. In my opinion, no one epitomizes this positivity more than Pharrell

---

[2] Are you a front-seater or back-seater?

[3] In other words, you may find yourself asking: How could the editors have ever allowed *this* to be published?

[4] The purpose of this chapter is not to say we Christians are to be legalistic and only listen to strictly "Christian" music, whether traditional or contemporary in style. I simply want us to see how the fear of God and fear of man play into everything around us. The songs listed are on my "playlist," but I want to point out how important it is for us Christians not to listen mindlessly to "clean" music and assume it does not affect our spiritual lives.

Williams. Always complimentary and encouraging, even when offering constructive thoughts, Pharrell oozes love for each person he meets. It's refreshing to see in a world becoming more negative by the day.

Calling himself "a Christian 'on paper' but a Universalist," Pharrell is not shy about his belief in God. He once said, "It's so incredibly arrogant and pompous. It's amazing that there are people who really believe that [God doesn't exist]. It's unbelievable." Further detailing his faith, Pharrell said, "Do I think that Christianity is the only way? No. I think the only route for everything is their connection to God. There's religious dogma that gets involved, something for the greater good and sometimes for not so great reasons . . . but they give you a way, a vehicle to get to God."

One of his most recognizable and widely acclaimed songs across all ages, "Happy," hit the top of popular music charts in over seventy-five countries around the world. "Happy" plays at a critical moment in the popular children's movie *Despicable Me 2*, which was nominated for an Academy Award in 2014. Easily the most recognizable song from the movie, "Happy" is now a children's book that depicts children across the world's cultures celebrating what it means to be happy. The children's book promotional concludes, "All the exuberance of the song pulses from these vibrant photographs of excited, happy kids. A keepsake and true classic in the making."

"Happy" is the first song on the soundtrack to our trip to the woods. As its easily recognizable introduction begins,[5] smiles break out on the bus, countenances rise, feet tap, and some even clap along as Pharrell sings the song's refrain for the first time, which includes the following lyric: "Clap along if you feel like happiness is the truth." A little further in the song Pharrell proclaims, "Here comes bad news . . . I'll be just fine" because "can't nothing bring me down."

Clean and innocuous, no? It's in a children's movie and in a children's book. Come on, Abraham! Well, let's take a closer look. This song implicitly speaks to the fear of man and the fear of God. Not seeing it? That's okay. Want to learn? Just clap along if you

---

[5] I can name that tune in two notes, George! Again, if you're like most Millennials, don't worry about this allusion.

feel like that's what you want to do. The lyrics certainly don't speak to a high fear of others. Any and all bad news—whether it's about the world outside of the singer or pointed criticisms of him—can't bring him down. He's so happy that such things don't matter. So, one of the two components of the fear of man is clearly very low.

However, the other component of the fear of man—the fear of self—is so high that nothing can bring it down. The song is so centered on personal happiness that it proclaims it as the truth. *Whoa, hold up!* Not only does that statement skyrocket the fear of man in the singer's Spiritual Fear Factor equation, it eliminates any fear of God, as well. As recorded in John 14:6, Jesus says, "I am the way, the truth, and the life. No one can come to the Father except through me." Jesus is the truth, not personal happiness. Joy and happiness are certainly fruit of an intimate relationship with Jesus Christ. However, personal happiness *is not* the truth. Jesus—and Jesus alone—*is* the truth.

Do you see it now? Or, should I say, do you hear it now? This is what our children are hearing not only from this song but from almost all others. What's the ultimate result if this is the mindset of our children as they grow up? A hedonistic, self-pleasure-seeking culture. Not surprisingly, it describes the contemporary Western world.

To illustrate the Spiritual Fear Factor of Pharrell's "Happy":

$$\text{Spiritual Fear Factor} = \frac{\text{Fear of God}}{\text{Fear of Man}} = \frac{\text{Fear of God}}{(\text{Fear of Others})(\text{Fear of Self})} = \frac{\downarrow}{\downarrow\uparrow} = \Downarrow$$

When looking at the underlying spiritual assumptions of what is seen as an immensely popular, positive, upbeat, and clean song, we see that it plants subtle seeds of a spirituality that reflects its writer and singer—a self-described "paper" Christian who does not hold to the foundational doctrine of Christianity of Jesus Christ being the only true way for salvation. I am reminded of Jesus telling the parable of the wheat and weeds:

> Here is another story Jesus told: "The Kingdom of Heaven is like a farmer who planted good seed in his field. [25] But that night as the workers slept, his

enemy came and planted weeds among the wheat, then slipped away. [26] When the crop began to grow and produce grain, the weeds also grew.

[27] "The farmer's workers went to him and said, 'Sir, the field where you planted that good seed is full of weeds! Where did they come from?'

[28] "'An enemy has done this!' the farmer exclaimed.

"'Should we pull out the weeds?' they asked.

[29] "'No,' he replied, 'you'll uproot the wheat if you do. [30] Let both grow together until the harvest. Then I will tell the harvesters to sort out the weeds, tie them into bundles, and burn them, and to put the wheat in the barn.'" (Matthew 13:24–30)

Good seeds and bad seeds. Intermingled. Slight distortions of the Truth, the ramifications of which are seen only after they're planted. Am I being too critical? A buzzkill, you may be saying? Way too overprotective and legalistic?

Maybe, but I want to stress again that if we are to apply what we learned in our recent history, language, biology, and math lessons to transform our lives biblically, we need to be as shrewd as snakes and harmless as doves.[6] Like I said, from what I've seen, I love Pharrell's attitude and personality. He's an Uplifter! In fact, I love Pharrell so much that I pray He will come to know that Jesus is the way, the truth, and the life. I love Pharrell so much that I pray He will follow Jesus, knowing that He is the only way to God. I love Pharrell so much that I pray someone speaks the truth in love[7]

---

[6] Jesus says in Matthew 10:16 (ESV): "Behold, I am sending you [His disciples during His earthly ministry and His disciples today] out as sheep in this midst of wolves, so be wise as serpents and innocent as doves."

[7] Ephesians 4:15: Instead, we [followers of Jesus Christ] will speak the truth in love, growing in every way more and more like Christ, who is the head of his body, the church.

(the same loving style that marks Pharrell's character) about a God he knows exists.

Two things will happen when someone shares the truth about Jesus in Pharrell's loving style: Gospel seeds will be planted in Pharrell's heart, and the follower of Jesus who is sharing will—through obedience—grow and mature in the fear of the Lord. That's what's called a win-win! Clap along if you feel like *that* is the truth!

Try

Coffee houses and acoustic music. The musical peanut butter and jelly sandwich of the twenty-first century. Two peas in a pod. Made for each other. Naturally, then, all on the bus are familiar when Colbie Caillat's popular song "Try" is the next and final song on our short bus trip's hit parade. Early in her career, Caillat remarked, "A lot of my fanbase is young girls from ten to twenty-five. So . . . I don't cuss onstage. I don't write songs about inappropriate things. If they're looking up to me . . . I don't want to be advising them to do things like that, so I just try to stay away from it." How refreshing to hear a pop star desire to be a positive role model! Hollywood, Nashville, and all places in between need more Colbie Caillats in that regard.

Like many of the younger generations, Caillat seems to be spiritual, yet irreligious. Research shows organized religion is declining, while spirituality is increasing. Almost 40 percent of those who claim no religion at the same time claim to be spiritual. It's understandable then to see the multi-Grammy-winning acoustic guitarist Caillat retweet "Absolutely" to a tweet of the Dalai Lama's famous quote, "Kindness is my religion."

With that background in mind, Caillat takes us behind-the-scenes in the writing and recording process for her smash hit "Try." Her website's biography states, "[Try] explains literally every step a woman takes to get herself ready to go out in public and how exhausting it is. There's so much [women] have to do in order to make [themselves] 'beautiful' [to] feel accepted in the public eye. This is an anthem for women to accept who they are and be comfortable showing it and not hiding it from one another."

If you've been paying attention, and if I'm at least a halfway decent communicator, it should be easy to spotlight that the fear of man—specifically the fear of others—is the central theme to "Try." Try not to become too chilled and relaxed while Caillat's guitar and piano lead you by your ears into the coffeehouse of your mind. Pay attention to the lyrics of "Try."

The song details the ways girls and women try to gain the acceptance of others in society. From masking themselves in layers of makeup, getting manicures and pedicures, styling their hair, going overboard at the gym, and keeping up with the fashion trends of the day to moving past modesty and values previously held, girls and women are disregarding the personal mental, emotional, financial, and spiritual effects of their actions. In our culture, they go to great lengths to perceive a sense of belonging and acceptance by others. That's the definition of fearing others in practice: letting others' opinions—above all else—drive and determine how you feel about yourself and what you will do to try and please them.

After pointing out the aforementioned strenuous lengths females are accustomed to going because of others, Caillat softly pivots while pointedly asking the question central to the theme of the song. She goes to the inward motivations that bear the outward actions. In my words, she asks, "Time out! Hold up! Why are we like this? Why do we care what others think of us?" *Hey, alright!* Minimize the fear of others. That's a positive message! I'm encouraged so far. However, the subsequent lyrical question wipes away any encouragement I have, from a spiritual standpoint. She asks, again in my own words, "Are you happy with yourself when nobody else is around?" *Uh, oh!* The flag of the fear of self raises above to shine above the land of not fearing others. This theme of "liking yourself the way you are" permeates the rest of the song. Ironically, Caillat concludes with the assuring affirmation that she likes you, despite the song's main idea of not caring what others think.

My question is whether the theme of "Try" is biblical. This may be where you are again thinking I'm making mountains out of molehills and am a legalistic jerk. Maybe I am, but before you put the book down, I want you to think about the Apostle Paul's words in Galatians 2:20 (ESV): "I have been crucified with Christ.

It is no longer I who live, but Christ who lives in me. And the life I now live in the flesh I live by faith in the Son of God, who loved me and gave himself for me."

Are we to like ourselves? Or, as followers of Jesus, are we to love the Son of God, who loved us so much He died for us? Are we to like us, or are we to love Jesus and be obedient to His Holy Spirit indwelling in us? Is it really about having a high self-esteem, or a high God-esteem?

Let's look at the Spiritual Fear Factor for Caillat's "Try":

$$\text{Spiritual Fear Factor} = \frac{\text{Fear of God}}{\text{Fear of Man}} = \frac{\text{Fear of God}}{(\text{Fear of Others})(\text{Fear of Self})} = \frac{\downarrow}{\downarrow\uparrow} = \Downarrow$$

Does it look familiar? It's exactly the same as Pharrell's "Happy." The self is elevated above God. The creation is above the Creator. The prophet Isaiah's words recorded in Isaiah 64:8 sound hollow next to the harmonies of "Try": "And yet, O LORD, you are our Father. We are the clay, and you are the potter. We all are formed by your hand." In Jeremiah's inspired prophecy, God's words spoken through Jeremiah to the nation of Israel and the people's response characterize us today:

> "Now, therefore, say to the men of Judah and the inhabitants of Jerusalem: 'Thus says the LORD, Behold, I am shaping disaster against you and devising a plan against you. Return, every one from his evil way, and amend your ways and your deeds.'

> "But they say, 'That is in vain! We will follow our own plans, and will every one act according to the stubbornness of his evil heart.'" (Jeremiah 18:11–12 (ESV))

God can't be any clearer, calling for repentance and obedience to fear Him more. Yet, people today, those who claim to be spiritual but irreligious, are doing what they want. They may not think what they are doing is evil; Caillat called writing and singing the song "liberating" because of its positive message. In this sense, worldly liberation leads to spiritual bondage. Perhaps an apt description of humanity is *Stubbornly Spiritual about Self.* That doesn't have quite the same connotation as "Happy" and "Try," but does it have the denotation of truth? As followers of Jesus, our answer must be in the affirmative.

Oh, look at that! Before realizing it, we've already arrived at our destination: the local nature preserve. Better get ready and put on your hiking boots before we meet our Guide!

Your James 1:22 Challenge

James writes to us, "But don't just listen to God's word. You must do what it says. Otherwise, you are only fooling yourselves." Use the following five prompts to apply lessons learned from this chapter centered on God's Word to transform your life.

1. What is your reaction to this chapter? Is Tim too harsh with his analysis? Why or why not?

2. What other songs have you heard that may have a positive message but, listening deeper, have a subtly small Spiritual Fear Factor?

3. Identify other types of media and aspects of today's world that—either overtly or subtly—impact the prism in which we view the world.

4. Compare having a high self-esteem and being crucified with Christ. How do they differ? Are the inward motivations and attitudes the same? Do the outward actions differ or look the same?

5. Prayerfully ask God to make you more sensitive to the subtleties of this world that, like a continuous small drip of water, can cause an enormous erosion of our faith before we ever realize it.

Chapter 8: Knowing the Names

"What's in a name? that which we call a rose
By any other name would smell as sweet."
-     Juliet, in William Shakespeare's *Romeo and Juliet*

"Therefore, God elevated him to the place of highest honor and gave him the name above all other names, that at the name of Jesus every knee should bow, in heaven and on earth and under the earth, and every tongue declare that Jesus Christ is Lord, to the glory of God the Father."
-     The Apostle Paul, Philippians 2:9–11

I f I were King of the World, everyone would wear nametags all the time. Think about it. Have you ever met someone for the first time and just seconds later already forgotten their name? Have you run into someone you first met only days ago and, attempting to remember their name, the hamster wheel in your mind spins so fast that the hamster flies off and gives you a headache? Maybe you're like me, where you don't want to take the chance of a social faux pas by calling someone by the wrong name, although you're 98 percent sure you know the correct one.[1]

Academic researchers[2] studied this phenomenon that crosses conversations and cultures. Their four-fold conclusion, in lay-men's terms as described the United Kingdom's *Daily Mail* is:

---

[1]   The fear of man in action.

[2]   Also known as: "People smarter than me"

1. Names hold little information, so the brain struggles to form a connection.

2. If the brain can't make connections, it's more likely to forget the data (in this case, the name).

3. The "next-in-line" effect also suggests that we fail to remember names because we are focusing on introducing ourselves.

4. Alternatively, if we're not interested in something, we tend to forget about it.

So, in today's culture, names in and of themselves don't mean much, so we don't care enough to remember them. Or, we're so focused on ourselves and what we're going to say, we don't remember what the other person is saying—if we even care about the person in the first place.

Contrast our culture with ancient culture described in Genesis 4:26: "When Seth grew up, he had a son and named him Enosh. At that time people first began to worship the LORD by name." Or with the psalmist's lyrics recorded in Psalm 148:13 (ESV), pertaining to all of creation: "Let them praise the name of the LORD, for his name alone is exalted; his majesty is above earth and heaven." God's name alone is to be praised and exalted. This means His name is worthy of our adoration and devotion, and will help us see who God is (Step #2 to fearing the Lord biblically).

Further, David sings to the Lord in Psalm 25:11 (ESV), "For your name's sake, O LORD, pardon my guilt, for it is great." David is asking God to forgive his sins to honor God's name. Is that the first thing you, as a follower of Jesus, think of when confessing your sins to God? That His name be glorified? Suddenly, the attention turns away from us and onto God—where it should be all along.

Maybe names are more important than we think. Let's try to remember God's name, as we introduce ourselves to Him after getting off our bus at the local nature preserve.

The Names of God in the Old Testament

In today's culture, a person may be named for a variety of reasons, including after a predecessor in the family, a man or woman in the Bible, or for many other reasons. But, if you spend time reading the historical account of the Old Testament, you will see that names hold a much more significant meaning. Names of people and places not only provided *identification*, but a special meaning to give the person or place a *sense of identity*. Names had a special meaning with a specific purpose. Given this, sixteen names of God found in the Old Testament reveal characteristics of His being, describing different, specific characteristics of the One, True, Living God we worship. The One we adore and to whom we are devoted. Come with me on a fast-paced hit parade of God's names found in the Old Testament.[3]

Think about it: Because God knows each of us individually by name, shouldn't we at least know His?

El Shaddai: Meaning "The All-Sufficient One, Lord God Almighty" in Hebrew. God—and only God—can supply, nourish, and truly satisfy us. He is our Sustainer. The Father sent His one and only Son, Jesus Christ, to die on the cross, paying the penalty for your sins and mine. Jesus then conquered death, rising on the third day, and then sent the Holy Spirit to live in the hearts of all believers.

Do you sense your dependence upon El Shaddai's sustaining presence in your life—from every breath you take to the smallest and largest details of your life?

El Elyon: "The Most High God" or "The Most Exalted God." In Psalm 57:2, David lyricizes, "I cry out to God Most High, to God who will fulfill his purpose for me." As we read the Old Testament,

---

[3]   It's like Casey Kasem or Ryan Seacrest, depending on your generation, counting down the Top 40 hits of the week. Sort of. Well, not really. But this countdown is way more important.

it's easy for us to understand what this means. Varying cultures during that time adopted many religions, which often demanded worship of many false gods and idols made out of earthly materials. It is more difficult for us to see today, but our false gods and idols include the love of money; the relentless pursuit of more pleasure, possessions, or prestige; our own good works, intelligence, athleticism, or beauty; and anything else that we value more than God. These are our idols.

Do you recognize idols in your life that are supplanting El Elyon, the Most High God?

Adonai: "Lord, Master." In Hebrew, this name of God is plural, which alludes to the Trinity—one God eternally existing in three persons: Father, Son, and Holy Spirit. Think about love for a second. For love to exist, there must be more than one person or thing. I can't love my wife if she doesn't exist. You can't "love" your favorite sports team or Hollywood star if they don't exist. You can't love God if He doesn't exist. There has to be one who loves and an object of that love. If God is love, and His characteristics are unchangeable, then an object of God's love must have always existed, too. Therefore, God existing as the Trinity is necessary for love to exist. Perhaps no greater example of the Trinity can be found than in the historical account of Jesus' baptism, when God the Father verbally affirms God the Son while God the Holy Spirit descends upon Him.[4] The One, True, Living, Triune God we worship strikingly differs from the gods of all other religions.

Do you see God as He truly is, Adonai, one God eternally existing in three persons?

---

[4] Matthew 3:16–17 (ESV): And when Jesus was baptized, immediately he went up from the water, and behold, the heavens were opened to him, and he saw the Spirit of God descending like a dove and coming to rest on him; [17] and behold, a voice from heaven said, "This is my beloved Son, with whom I am well pleased."

Yahweh: "Lord, Jehovah" or "I AM!" Revealed by God Himself in Exodus 3, Yahweh is by far the most used name of God—over 6,000 times! The promised name of God, Yahweh denotes God's omnipotence—His absolute and unlimited great power. It's a proper name built out of the word meaning "I AM," reminding us God absolutely was, is, and is to come. In Exodus 3:15, God tells Moses, "Say this to the people of Israel: Yahweh, the God of your ancestors—the God of Abraham, the God of Isaac, and the God of Jacob—has sent me to you. This is my eternal name, my name to remember for all generations." Generations of Jews to this day—out of reverent, godly fear—will not even write out this name of God out of a fear of using His name in vain. With that in mind, it's no wonder Jesus shocks the unbelieving Jews as recorded in John 8:58: "Jesus answered, 'I tell you the truth, before Abraham was even born, I AM!'" The Old Testament God who sealed up Noah in the ark, who called Abraham, who spoke to Moses in the burning bush, who wrote the Ten Commandments, who could not be seen face-to-face, chose to show Himself face-to-face with humanity as fully God and fully human in Jesus Christ and His mission to save and redeem mankind.

Do you see Jesus for who He truly was, is, and is to come—Yahweh—"I AM!"?

Jehovah Nissi: "The Lord My Banner." Used once in the Bible,[5] this name of God, *Nissi*, is derived from the Hebrew word *Nes*, which means "banner." During the time period of the Old Testament, warring nations would fly their flag on a pole on their respective front lines. The flag, a focal point, roused feelings of hope. Continuing today, our God—Jehovah Nissi—is a banner for us to focus on for encouragement and hope.

Are you living in such a way that Jehovah Nissi is flying above your heart and pointing others to Him?

---

[5] Exodus 17:5 (ESV): And the LORD said to Moses, "Pass on before the people, taking with you some of the elders of Israel, and take in your hand the staff with which you struck the Nile, and go."

129

Jehovah-Raah: "The Lord my Shepherd" or "The Lord my Friend." God continually reveals Himself to us and desires intimacy with us. We are to follow God by faith in Jesus Christ and through the promptings of the Holy Spirit, just as a sheep follows its shepherd. Infinitely better than your "best friend," God wants nothing more than a deeper relationship with you.

How do you see God: As a distant, uncaring god who is always disappointed in you or as an intimate, loving Shepherd and Friend—Jehovah-Raah?

Jehovah Rapha: "The Lord That Heals." God is the Great Physician, who heals the spiritual, emotional, and physical needs of His people. Many biblical accounts record a man or woman having simple faith in Jesus, which results in their physical and, more importantly, spiritual healing. God provides miraculous physical and spiritual healing today. During the advent season, we approach the time of the greatest healing procedure in history: God sending His Son, Jesus Christ, to earth to heal us by taking the penalty and paying the debt of our sins.

Do you have faith in Jehovah Rapha to heal you spiritually for all eternity through faith in Jesus Christ?

Jehovah Shammah: "The Lord is There." Used only in Ezekiel 48:35,[6] Jehovah Shammah symbolically represents the earthly Jerusalem that God will restore for Jesus Christ's millennial reign, prophetically seen in Revelation 20:4.[7] As followers of Jesus, we

---

[6] Ezekiel 48:35 (ESV): The circumference of the city shall be 18,000 cubits [approximately 6 miles]. And the name of the city from that time on shall be, The Lord Is There."

[7] Revelation 20:4: Then I saw thrones, and the people sitting on them had been given the authority to judge. And I saw the souls of those who had been beheaded for their testimony about Jesus and for proclaiming the word of God. They had not worshiped the beast or his statue, nor accepted his mark on their foreheads or their hands. They all came to life again, and they reigned with Christ for a thousand years.

always have God with us because the Holy Spirit indwells in our hearts. The Apostle Paul rhetorically asks early followers of Jesus, "Don't you realize that your body is the temple of the Holy Spirit, who lives in you and was given to you by God?"[8]

What does it mean to you knowing that, as a follower of Jesus, God gives His Holy Spirit to be "templed" and live inside you—that Jehovah Shammah is always right there with you?

Jehovah Tsidkenu: "The Lord Our Righteousness." Used only twice by the prophet Jeremiah,[9] Jehovah Tsidkenu is the name by which Israel and God's kingdom will be named. As followers of Jesus, God is our righteousness because Jesus paid the penalty of our sins through His death, burial, and resurrection. God sees those who place their faith in Jesus Christ righteous because of Him, unstained by their sin. The prophet Zechariah describes a symbolic picture of this transformation from being clothed and seen in our sin's filth to being adorned in God's righteousness:

> Then the angel showed me Jeshua the high priest standing before the angel of the LORD. The Accuser, Satan, was there at the angel's right hand, making accusations against Jeshua. ² And the LORD said to Satan, "I, the LORD, reject your accusations, Satan. Yes, the LORD, who has chosen Jerusalem, rebukes you. This man is like a burning stick that has been snatched from the fire."
>
> ³ Jeshua's clothing was filthy as he stood there before the angel. ⁴ So the angel said to the others standing

---

8   1 Corinthians 6:19

9   Jeremiah 23:6 (ESV): In his days Judah will be saved, and Israel will dwell securely. And this is the name by which he will be called: 'The LORD is our righteousness.'

Jeremiah 33:16 (ESV): In those days Judah will be saved, and Israel will dwell securely. And this is the name by which it will be called: 'The LORD is our righteousness.'

there, "Take off his filthy clothes." And turning to Jeshua he said, "See, I have taken away your sins, and now I am giving you these fine new clothes."

⁵ Then I said, "They should also place a clean turban on his head." So they put a clean priestly turban on his head and dressed him in new clothes while the angel of the LORD stood by. (Zechariah 3:1–5)

Remember God upgrading Adam and Eve's clothes to meet their short-term needs? Here, God gives us new clothes to wear for all eternity! What clothes are you wearing: Old filthy rags stained in sin and made by Satan, or the finest, newest clothes in all of creation courtesy of Jehovah Tsidkenu?

Jehovah Mekoddishkem: "The Lord Who Sanctifies You" or "The Lord Who Makes Holy." Used only twice by Moses,[10] Jehovah Mekoddishkem reveals God's sanctification—or setting apart—of His people as holy. In the Old Testament, God covenants and sets apart the Israelites, making Him their God and them His people.[11] Today, as followers of Jesus, God sets us apart from the world while we still live in it. We previously learned this in back in biology class, but for extra credit, make sure you read the upcoming footnotes to see the author of Hebrews writing in chapter 8, verses 8–10,[12] of

---

[10] Exodus 31:3: I have filled him with the Spirit of God, giving him great wisdom, ability, and expertise in all kinds of crafts.
Leviticus 20:8 (ESV): Keep my statutes and do them; I am the LORD who sanctifies you.

[11] Exodus 6:7 (ESV): I will take you to be my people, and I will be your God, and you shall know that I am the LORD your God, who has brought you out from under the burdens of the Egyptians.

[12] Hebrews 8:8–10 (ESV): For he finds fault with them when he says: "Behold, the days are coming, declares the Lord, when I will establish a new covenant with the house of Israel and with the house of Judah, ⁹ not like the covenant that I made with their fathers on the day when I took them by the hand to bring them out of the land of Egypt. For they did not continue in my covenant, and

his letter wherein he refers back to the prophet Jeremiah's words recorded in Jeremiah 31:31–34.[13] Peter writes in 1 Peter 2:9, "But you are a chosen race, a royal priesthood, a holy nation, a people for His own possession, that you may proclaim the excellencies of Him who called you out of darkness into His marvelous light."

Do you praise Jehovah Mekoddishkem, proclaiming His moral virtues and thanking Him for saving and sanctifying you?

El Olam: "The Everlasting God" or "The Eternal God." First used in Genesis 21:33 when Abraham plants a grove in Beersheba after covenanting with Abimelech, the name El Olam reveals God's eternal character—not simply years past to years future, but eternity past to eternity future. The same God who created the heavens and earth; who promised Abraham as many descendants as the stars in the sky, every one of which He created; who chose Israel as His people; who sent His only Son, Jesus, to save us by dying in our place on the cross to pay the penalty of our sins; who sends the Holy Spirit to comfort, guide, and indwell those who follow Jesus, is the same God we worship, serve, and pray to every day! As the pages of history turn from day to day, week to week, month to month, and year to year, may we be found praising our

---

so I showed no concern for them, declares the Lord. [10] For this is the covenant that I will make with the house of Israel after those days, declares the Lord: I will put my laws into their minds, and write them on their hearts, and I will be their God, and they shall be my people.

[13] Jeremiah 31:31–34 (ESV): "Behold, the days are coming, declares the LORD, when I will make a new covenant with the house of Israel and the house of Judah, [32] not like the covenant that I made with their fathers on the day when I took them by the hand to bring them out of the land of Egypt, my covenant that they broke, though I was their husband, declares the LORD. [33] For this is the covenant that I will make with the house of Israel after those days, declares the LORD: I will put my law within them, and I will write it on their hearts. And I will be their God, and they shall be my people. [34] And no longer shall each one teach his neighbor and each his brother, saying, 'Know the LORD,' for they shall all know me, from the least of them to the greatest, declares the LORD. For I will forgive their iniquity, and I will remember their sin no more."

everlasting God for being the God of Ancient Days; the God of the Universe; and the God of today, tomorrow, and eternity!

Speaking in purely human terms on this side of eternity, do you realize that we cannot yet fully realize the eternal nature of El Olam?

Elohim: "God," "Judge," or "Creator." First used in Genesis 1:1 when God creates the heaven and the earth, Elohim refers specifically to the LORD God of Israel. Elohim is the second-most used name in the Old Testament to describe God. He first created everything in eternity past and, on a day to come, will make all things new again for eternity future.[14]

When you look at nature and other human beings, do you see and love them as Elohim's creation?

Qanna: "Jealous, Zealous." Our God is a jealous God. At first, this characteristic seems to have a negative connotation, but we know that God is perfect. So, what characteristic of God does Qanna convey? As the Blue Letter Bible team of biblical scholars write: "The fundamental meaning relates to a marriage relationship. God is depicted as Israel's husband; He is a jealous God, wanting all our praise for Himself and no one else." Just as God is depicted as Israel's husband, so the corporate church is depicted as the bride of Jesus Christ.

Could your love for Jesus be described as Qanna's love for you?

Jehovah Jireh: "The Lord Will Provide." A father's love for his only son, a son promised by God, a son commanded to be sacrificed for God—what combination of faith, doubt, and torment must Abraham be experiencing as he treks up Mount Moriah. Faith is telling him God will keep His covenant. Doubt is questioning how

---

[14] Revelation 21:5 (ESV): And he who was seated on the throne said, "Behold, I am making all things new." Also he said, "Write this down, for these words are trustworthy and true."

it can be fulfilled if He sacrifices his only son, Isaac. Killing your own son? The word "torturous" or any other word cannot conceive of the emotion. Most of us know how the story unfolds. After tying Isaac to the altar and raising his knife to kill him, Abraham is stopped by the angel of the LORD who tells him not to harm his son, Isaac, in any way. Why? In the angel's own words: "For now I know that you truly fear God." God tests Abraham's heart to see if Abraham fears Him. And, God only knows how Abraham felt, because, unlike Abraham, God sacrificed His Son for you and for me. Used only in Genesis 22:14,[15] Abraham gives Mount Moriah the name Jehovah Jireh to symbolically represent God interceding for Him—as Jesus intercedes for us—to provide a suitable sacrifice that was not Isaac in Abraham's titanic test of faith.

Are you trusting Jehovah Jireh to provide for all your physical and spiritual needs?

Jehovah Shalom: "The Lord is Peace." Gideon builds an altar and names it Jehovah Shalom after realizing an angel of the Lord appeared to him face-to-face. The angel's message to Gideon? In my own words: "God is with you, so go and lead the rescue of the Israelites from a seven-year, terror-filled reign of an enemy so cruel that the Israelites are starving." Gideon, to memorialize the place God spoke to him through the angel, names the altar Jehovah Shalom. God brings peace to the Israelites through Gideon's military leadership. Gideon rightfully tells his fellow countrymen that it was not him who brought victory and peace, but God Himself. The Apostle Paul pens a profound passage on peace to the Philippian church. He exhorts:

> Don't worry about anything; instead, pray about everything. Tell God what you need, and thank him for all he has done. [7] Then you will experience God's peace, which exceeds anything we can

---

[15] Genesis 22:14 (ESV): So Abraham called the name of that place, "The LORD will provide"; as it is said to this day, "On the mount of the LORD it shall be provided."

understand. His peace will guard your hearts and minds as you live in Christ Jesus.

[8] And now, dear brothers and sisters, one final thing. Fix your thoughts on what is true, and honorable, and right, and pure, and lovely, and admirable. Think about things that are excellent and worthy of praise. [9] Keep putting into practice all you learned and received from me—everything you heard from me and saw me doing. Then the God of peace will be with you. (Philippians 4:6–9)

Look at what we are called to do and what God will do. We are not to worry but pray, which includes asking God for what we need and thanking Him for all He's done. God will then give us an incomprehensible blessing of peace that will guard our hearts and minds. It's this God-given peace that God uses to guard our spiritual lives. Then, God commands us through Paul to fix our thoughts (also translated to "meditate") on things that are excellent and worthy of praise, including what is true, honorable, right, pure, lovely, and admirable. Where's the best source for all these excellent and praiseworthy things? God's Word, the Bible. Joshua strongly commands and urges the Israelites to do so with God's law and for us to do so now with the Bible:

Be strong and very courageous. Be careful to obey all the instructions Moses gave you. Do not deviate from them, turning either to the right or to the left. Then you will be successful in everything you do. [8] Study this Book of Instruction continually. Meditate on it day and night so you will be sure to obey everything written in it. Only then will you prosper and succeed in all you do. (Joshua 1:7–8)

See the similarities between Joshua and Paul's exhortations?

Meditating involves much more than simply thinking. It means to be *continually considering*. We aren't called only to meditate, though, we are called to then *put into practice* what we've learned.[16] We have to *think* and *act* for the God of peace to be with us. This sounds a lot like our definition of fearing God, which includes seeing, believing, and then responding through our actions.

Do your preoccupations and worries overshadow your prayers and witness of Jehovah Shalom?

Jehovah Sabaoth: "The Lord of Hosts" or "The Lord of Powers." Espionage. Secret agents. Good guys turned bad that turn out to be good in the end. Hollywood eats these plots and spits out movie after movie. Yet, Hollywood cannot write a better story than God's prophet Elisha, who tells the king of Israel the military strategies of the enemy Arameans. The king of Aram becomes so infuriated that he summons his own military leaders together only to accuse them of treachery. Their reply? "Elisha, the prophet in Israel, tells the king of Israel even the words you speak in the privacy of your bedroom!"[17] To no one's surprise, the king of Aram finds out where Elisha is and sends his army after him. As the vast Aramean army surrounds Elisha, Elisha's servant runs to alert him. Note Elisha's first words as we pick up the narrative:

> "Don't be afraid!" Elisha told him. "For there are more on our side than on theirs!" [17] Then Elisha prayed, "O LORD, open his eyes and let him see!" The LORD opened the young man's eyes, and when he looked up, he saw that the hillside around Elisha was filled with horses and chariots of fire.
>
> [18] As the Aramean army advanced toward him, Elisha prayed, "O LORD, please make them blind."

---

[16] Do our *James 1:22 Challenges* ring a bell?

[17] 2 Kings 6:12b

> So the LORD struck them with blindness as Elisha
> had asked. (2 Kings 6:16–18)

Elisha then leads the Arameans to the middle of Samaria, right into the hands of the Israeli army. However, when the king of Israel asks what to do, Elisha—foreshadowing sinners saved by grace feasting with Jesus in Heaven—showers mercy upon the Arameans by ordering a large feast to be prepared for them before allowing their return to the king of Aram. Such was the last time the Arameans attempted to raid Israel.

God's sovereignty extends over both the physical and spiritual armies—all armies of the heavens and the earth. His sovereignty enables spying spiritually, encamping spiritual armies, eliciting physical perplexities, and entreating marauders mercifully. *Nothing is beyond God!*

Living today, with wars and rumors of wars,[18] do you elevate Jehovah Sabaoth to His rightful place above any human or spiritual army standing to battle against you?

From Old to New

We've counted down sixteen names of God given in the Old Testament to reveal His unique character. It's only fitting then that the Old Testament prophet Isaiah leads us into the break with these words to Ahaz, the king of Judah at the time: "All right then, the Lord himself will give you the sign. Look! The virgin will conceive a child! She will give birth to a son and will call him Immanuel (which means 'God is with us')."[19] Isaiah continues to provide hope for Israel later when he prophesizes, "For a child is born to us, a son is given to us. The government will rest on his shoulders. And

---

[18] Jesus says in Matthew 24:6 (ESV): "And you will hear of wars and rumors of wars. See that you are not alarmed, for this must take place, but the end is not yet." My reaction to this statement? Don't panic. Don't fear. Jesus wins in the end!

[19] Isaiah 7:14

he will be called: Wonderful Counselor, Mighty God, Everlasting Father, Prince of Peace."[20]

When we return to continue the introduction to God, our Guide, we'll consider the names given to Him in the New Testament. See you on the flip side after this section break!

The Names of God in the New Testament

Welcome back! Isaiah prophesies about Jesus Christ, adorning Him with the name Immanuel, which means "God with us." Jesus Christ, fully God, came to earth, fully human, to walk and talk among us, to give us an example of how to live, to give us hope for tomorrow, to give us victory over death, and to give us life eternal.

An entire volume can be written describing the 200-plus names ascribed to Jesus Christ whose ministry is recorded in the New Testament. Each attributes a characteristic unique to Him, and all merit further study. I encourage you to find a reputable biblical resource to introduce yourself to Jesus in a way you may not have previously—through His names.

With that said, it is important to delve into greater detail regarding one name of Jesus because we've been using it throughout our journey together. Throughout his earthly ministry, Jesus retreats from the large crowds following Him to pray. God the Son routinely and customarily converses with God the Father through prayer.[21] His ministry is marked by prayer. No other true ministry exists without prayer. With only His twelve closest disciples with Him at the time, Jesus asks them a simple question: "Who does everyone think I am?" Their response, as recorded by an inquisitive, detail-oriented, and analytical doctor named Luke follows:

> "Well," they replied, "some say John the Baptist, some say Elijah, and others say you are one of the other ancient prophets risen from the dead."

---

[20] Isaiah 9:6

[21] How much more then do you and I need to pray? #convicted

[20] Then he asked them, "But who do you say I am?"

Peter replied, "You are the Messiah sent from God!" (Luke 9:19–20)

The Hebrew name *Messiah* and the Greek name *Christ* both mean "anointed one." Jesus Christ is the Messiah, anointed by God to be the Savior of Israel and all who believe and follow Him as their Savior and Lord. There would be no hope if Jesus wasn't anointed by God. But Jesus is. There would be no hope if Jesus wasn't the perfect sacrifice. But Jesus is. There would be no hope if Jesus did not defeat death. But Jesus does.[22] There would be no freedom if Jesus could not be our Lord. But Jesus is.

Born Shadrach Meshach Lockridge in 1913 in Texas, Dr. S. M. Lockridge came to be, as described by the *Los Angeles Times*, "a major religious and social force in San Diego for decades," known for his "evangelical conferences, powerful preaching, and civil rights activism." Having served on the faculty of the Billy Graham School of Evangelism and the Greater Los Angeles Sunday School Convention, this son of a preacher began his ministry in 1940 and served as a pastor in San Diego beginning in 1952. Dr. Lockridge's ministry included serving as pastor of Calvary Baptist Church and president of the California Missionary Baptist State Convention.

The year is 1976. The city is Detroit. The congregation is packed and overflowing. And the Holy Spirit is at work through Dr. Lockridge, as he preaches what is simply now known as *That's My King*:

My King was born King.

The Bible says He's a Seven-Way King.
He's the King of the Jews—that's a racial King.
He's the King of Israel—that's a national King.
He's the King of righteousness.
He's the King of the ages.

---

[22] 1 Corinthians 15:57: But thank God! He gives us victory over sin and death through our Lord Jesus Christ.

He's the King of Heaven.
He's the King of glory.
He's the King of kings,
And He is the Lord of lords.

Now that's my King! Well I wonder if you know Him.
Do you know Him?

Don't try to mislead me.
Do you know my King?

David said the Heavens declare the glory of God,
And the firmament showeth His handiwork.
My King is the only one whom there are no means of measure
that can define His limitless love.
No far seeing telescope can bring into visibility the coastline
of His shoreless supplies.
No barriers can hinder Him from pouring out His blessing.

Well, well,
He's enduringly strong.
He's entirely sincere.
He's eternally steadfast.
He's immortally graceful.
He's imperially powerful.
He's impartially merciful.
That's my King!

He's God's Son.
He's the sinner's Savior.
He's the Centerpiece of civilization.
He stands alone in Himself.
He's august.
He's unique.
He's unparalleled.

He's unprecedented.
He's supreme.
He's pre-eminent.

Well, He's the loftiest idea in literature.
He's the highest personality in philosophy.
He's the supreme problem in higher criticism.
He's the fundamental doctrine of true theology.
He's the cardinal necessity of spiritual religion.
That's my King!

He's the miracle of the age.
He's the superlative of everything good that you choose to call Him.

Well, He's the only one able to supply all of our needs simultaneously.
He supplies strength for the weak.
He's available for the tempted and the tried.
He sympathizes and He saves.
He's strong and He guides.
He heals the sick.
He cleanses the lepers.
He forgives sinners.
He discharges debtors.
He delivers the captives.
He defends the feeble.
He blesses the young.
He serves the unfortunate.
He regards the aged.
He rewards the diligent and He beautifies the meek.
Do you know Him?

Well, my King is a King of knowledge.
He's the Wellspring of wisdom.
He's the Doorway of deliverance.
He's the Pathway of peace.

He's the Roadway of righteousness.
He's the Highway of holiness.
He's the Gateway of glory.
He's the Master of the mighty.
He's the Captain of the conquerors.
He's the Head of the heroes.
He's the Leader of the legislators.
He's the Overseer of the overcomers.
He's the Governor of governors.
He's the Prince of princes.
He's the King of kings and He's the Lord of lords.

That's my King! Yeah! Yeah!
That's my King! My King, yeah!

His office is manifold.
His promise is sure.
His light is matchless.
His goodness is limitless.
His mercy is everlasting.
His love never changes.
His word is enough.
His grace is sufficient.
His reign is righteous.
His yoke is easy and His burden is light.

Well, I wish I could describe Him to you,
But He's indescribable.
He's indescribable. Yeah!

He's incomprehensible.
He's invincible.
He's irresistible.

I'm trying to tell you,
The heavens of heavens cannot contain Him,
Let alone a man explain Him.

You can't get Him out of your mind.
You can't get Him off of your hand.
You can't outlive Him and you can't live without Him.

Well, Pharisees couldn't stand Him,
But they found out they couldn't stop Him.
Pilate couldn't find any fault in Him.
The witnesses couldn't get their testimonies to agree.
Herod couldn't kill Him.
Death couldn't handle Him and the grave couldn't hold Him.

That's my King! Yeah!

He always has been and He always will be.
I'm talking about He had no predecessor,
And He'll have no successor.
There was nobody before Him,
And there'll be nobody after Him.
You can't impeach Him,
And He's not going to resign.
That's my King! That's my King!

Thine, Thine is the kingdom and the power and the glory.
Well, all the power belongs to my King.
We're around here talking about black power and white power
and green power,
But it's God's power. Thine is the power.

Yeah!
And the glory.
We try to get prestige and honor and glory for ourselves,
But the glory is all His. Yes!
Thine is the Kingdom,
And the power and the glory,
Forever and ever,
And ever,
And ever.

How long is that?
And ever and ever and ever and ever.
And when you get through with all of the forevers,
Then, Amen!

Echoing the late Dr. S. M. Lockridge, I simply ask: Do you know Jesus? Do you know Dr. Lockridge's King? Do you know my King? Well, I wonder if you know Him. Do you know Him?

Your James 1:22 Challenge

James writes to us, "But don't just listen to God's word. You must do what it says. Otherwise, you are only fooling yourselves." Use the following five prompts to apply lessons learned from this chapter centered on God's Word to transform your life.

1. Were you or people in your family named after someone or for a particular reason? If you've named a child, why did you choose the name you did?

2. Do you understand the difference between a name providing *identification* (like today's names) and providing a *sense of identity* (as names in the Old Testament do)?

3. Reread the questions at the end of the respective paragraphs for each of the names of God in the Old Testament. Prayerfully meditate on your answers. Write down your thoughts on each unique name. Had you heard of that particular name before? When have you seen the particular characteristic in God in your life or in others'?

4. Research some of the 200-plus names of Jesus. Which names stick out to you? Write down your thoughts in response to what you learn.

5. What parts of Dr. Lockridge's *That's My King* resonate with you? Why? Try listening to a recording of *That's My*

King, whether it's simply an audio recording or a very popular "lyric video" that can be found on the Internet.

Chapter 9: Walking in the World

"Specifically, we need to realize that all the things we do here—
from the academics to the extracurricular activities—don't matter.
Really. They don't matter at all. The tests don't matter. The intern-
ships don't matter. The activities don't matter. Nothing students do
at this school matters."

- Dashiell F. Young-Saver, Harvard Class of 2016, in
  Harvard's *Crimson* student newspaper

"Every single thing you do matters. You have been created as one
of a kind. You have been created in order to make a difference. You
have within you the power to change the world."

- Andy Andrews, author of *The Butterfly Effect: How Your
  Life Matters*

New England winters are tough.[1] Snow drifts abound after
blizzards. All ages of the toughest, most skilled athletes—
hockey players—play on frozen ponds indoors and out.[2] Some
of America's most prestigious universities are separated by mere
miles in Boston, Massachusetts.

In 1941, a mild-mannered professor, Edward Lorenz, steps
away from his computer to get some coffee inside the halls of the
Massachusetts Institute of Technology on a New England winter's

---

[1] Alaskans, Canadians, and Russians disagree.

[2] No debate necessary about the toughest, most-skilled athletes. I currently have
the power of the pen. And, while I'm at it: *Let's Go Boston Bruins!* I was
determined to get that in here somewhere.

day. Little does he know that when he returns, he'll change the course of history, science, and philosophy. That year, the *Butterfly Effect* was born; in it, Lorenz posited that "the flap of a butterfly's wings might ultimately cause a tornado."

It took some thirty years for Lorenz's theory to rapidly gain ascension and approval in the academic realms of meteorology, geology, and biology. It underpinned science's *Chaos Theory*. Steven Strogatz, a professor of applied mathematics at Cornell University, says, "It was philosophically very shocking. Determinism[3] was equated with predictability before Lorenz. After Lorenz, we came to see that determinism might give you short-term predictability, but in the long run, things could be unpredictable. That's what we associate with the word 'chaos.'"

Fifty-four years after Lorenz's coffee trip, Chris Rosati sits in a Durham, North Carolina, diner. Living with ALS but wondering if the *Butterfly Effect* translates from physics to kindness, Rosati sees two young girls at the table next to him. *Just how far could one act of kindness go?* Rosati gives sisters thirteen-year-old Cate and ten-year-old Anna Cameron each one $50 bill with a simple instruction: *Do something kind.* The sisters can only stare in disbelief after this act of a complete stranger. Admittedly, the memory of the act fades in Rosati's mind until he receives an email with pictures of an African village with many of its natives holding signs reading: "Thanks a lot for spreading kindness, Chris Rosati."

Knowing of this village in Sierra Leone because of their father's work in the Peace Corps, Cate and Anna decided to throw a feast because—after years of hard work to fight the deadly Ebola disease—the village was finally Ebola-free.

Later, speaking of his social experiment proving *The Butterfly Effect*, Rosati reflects, "Oh man. You get a whole lot of butterflies to flap their wings."

---

[3] Without getting too technical, *Determinism* is the theory that concludes that acts of the will, occurrences in nature, or social or psychological phenomena are causally (not casually!) determined by preceding events or natural laws.

Standing at the Edge of the Nature Preserve

How appropriate that, after being properly introduced to our Guide, we see butterflies in the nature preserve we're about to enter. As part of our education in the Lab of Life, together we'll discover different spiritual paths—paths that differ greatly.

One is straight and narrow. Two are crooked.

One is brightly lit. Two are darkly dim.

One is smooth, enabling us to walk with ease. Two are full of stumbling blocks, causing us to trip and fall.

One is peaceful. Two are full of fearing harm.

One is delightful and satisfying. Two are disappointing.

One is refreshing. Two are tiresome.

One is full of wisdom. Two are full of wickedness.

One is wholesome. Two are devious.

One is good. Two are evil.

One is walked by those knowing where to go. Two are walked by those who don't even know what they're stumbling over.

One is walked by the innocent. Two are walked by the guilty.

One leads up to life. Two lead down to death.

One is marked by the fear of the Lord. Two are marked by the abhorrence of Him.

Remember, God is our Guide. One by one, He hands each of us the following map based on the five wisdom books of the Bible: Job, Psalms, Proverbs, Ecclesiastes, and Song of Solomon. The map's purpose? To help us navigate the nature preserve in the Lab of Life, which really is every day of our lives. Let's take a look and study it together:

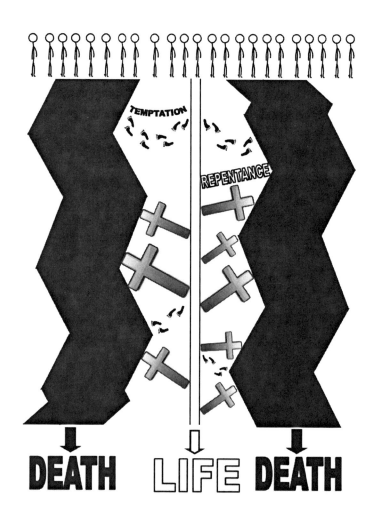

The Crossroads

Each day, multiple times a day, we stand with many spiritual paths on which we can walk, based on our thoughts, attitudes, emotions, and actions. All have consequences. King Solomon says, "A wise person chooses the right road; a fool takes the wrong one."[4]

God, speaking through the prophet Jeremiah as recorded in Jeremiah 6:16, tells Judah and us, "Stop at the crossroads and look around. Ask for the old, godly way, and walk in it. Travel its path, and you will find rest for your souls. But you reply, 'No, that's not the road we want!'"

The Hebrew word for "crossroads" not only means a physical road or path, but figuratively a way of life or of one's character. Did you notice the Lord doesn't say "crossroad," but instead "crossroads?" That's plural—meaning more than one. Becoming justified by grace through faith in Jesus Christ is the first of many crossroads in a Christian's life, the process of which is sanctification. Sanctification—growing and maturing spiritually to be more like Jesus—is not a cake-walk. It's full of ups and downs. It's full of choices. Contrary to what some may believe, becoming a follower of Jesus doesn't make life easier; it makes life harder.

God commands us to ask Him to show us the right path. In fact, sometimes we come up to a path and think it's the right course to take, but it's not. Both Proverbs 14:12 and 16:25 say: "There is a path before each person that seems right, but it ends in death." For this warning to be included twice in the one of the Bible's books of wisdom means we need to pay special attention. But, how then are we to know which path to take? Look back at Jeremiah's words. God's command is to ask Him. We already became familiar with these verses in language class, but they bear repeating now:

> Trust in the LORD with all your heart; do not depend on your own understanding. [6] Seek his will in all you do, and he will show you which path to take. (Proverbs 3:5–6)

---

[4] Ecclesiastes 10:2

How do we ask God and seek His will? By reading His Word (the Bible), by listening and talking to Him (through prayer), and by following the promptings of the Holy Spirit (with God-given wisdom and discernment).

In the book of Psalms, we see God's Word describe the foundation of true wisdom. Guess what it is? The fear of the Lord.[5] King Solomon repeats this fact in Proverbs 9:10 (ESV): "The fear of the LORD is the beginning of wisdom, and the knowledge of the Holy One is insight." Earlier in Proverbs, Solomon tells us that the fear of the Lord is also the beginning of knowledge.[6]

The Book of Job recounts the faithfulness of a God-fearing man of the same name. God allowed Satan to take anything and everything away from Job—from his many possessions, his family, his health, and his reputation—except for his life. Satan wrongly thinks Job will curse God after all these atrocities. Even after the encouragement of his wife to curse God, Job doesn't. Instead, Job *questions* God. And, when God answers, Job fears Him more than ever before. Amidst his horrible suffering, Job cries aloud:

> But do people know where to find wisdom? Where can they find understanding? [13] No one knows where to find it, for it is not found among the living. [14] "It is not here," says the ocean. "Nor is it here," says the sea. [15] It cannot be bought with gold. It cannot be purchased with silver. [16] It's worth more than all the gold of Ophir, greater than precious onyx or lapis lazuli. [17] Wisdom is more valuable than gold and crystal. It cannot be purchased with jewels mounted in fine gold. [18] Coral and jasper are worthless in trying to get it. The price of wisdom is far above rubies. [19] Precious

---

[5] Psalm 111:10 (ESV): The fear of the LORD is the beginning of wisdom; all those who practice it have a good understanding. His praise endures forever!

[6] Proverbs 1:7a (ESV): The fear of the LORD is the beginning of knowledge;

peridot from Ethiopia cannot be exchanged for it. It's worth more than the purest gold.

20 But do people know where to find wisdom? Where can they find understanding? 21 It is hidden from the eyes of all humanity. Even the sharp-eyed birds in the sky cannot discover it. 22 Destruction and Death say, "We've heard only rumors of where wisdom can be found."

23 God alone understands the way to wisdom; he knows where it can be found, 24 for he looks throughout the whole earth and sees everything under the heavens. 25 He decided how hard the winds should blow and how much rain should fall. 26 He made the laws for the rain and laid out a path for the lightning. 27 Then he saw wisdom and evaluated it. He set it in place and examined it thoroughly. 28 And this is what he says to all humanity: "The fear of the Lord is true wisdom; to forsake evil is real understanding." (Job 28:12–28)

True wisdom *can't* be found only by human means. True wisdom *can't* be bought with even the purest gold. True wisdom *can't* be comprehended by Satan and evil. However, true wisdom *can* be understood by God. True wisdom *can* be found by God. True wisdom *can* be studied thoroughly by God. True wisdom *is God*.

And after Job's close examination of true wisdom, he concludes in Job 28:28 with God's words (my paraphrase): "The fear of me—the I AM—is true wisdom. True understanding is then to forsake evil." After seeing who we are, like Job does, which is Step #1 of our definition of fearing the Lord, Job identifies Steps 2–4: We see God for who He is; what He has done, is doing, and will do; and we respond in obedience to Him. We fear God biblically by:

1. Seeing who we are.
2. Seeing who God is.

3. Believing what God has done, is doing, and will do.
4. Responding in obedience to God.

Solomon sums it up this way:

> Guard your heart above all else, for it determines
> the course of your life. . . . [25] Look straight ahead,
> and fix your eyes on what lies before you. [26] Mark
> out a straight path for your feet; stay on the safe
> path. [27] Don't get sidetracked; keep your feet from
> following evil. (Proverbs 4:23, 25–27)

Every day, we have multiple opportunities in life to choose
our innermost thoughts and attitudes—the most central, core part
of our being, our heart, and then how we act as a result. We can
spiritually walk in wisdom by fearing God, or we can walk away
from Him. May we follow in Job's footsteps, in lockstep with
Solomon's admonition, living with true wisdom by fearing the
Lord, and acting out of an understanding of and obedience to God
by avoiding evil.

The Straight and Narrow

By now, if you didn't sleep through our earlier classes, you
have a pretty good idea of what it means to fear the Lord. To review
one more time, fearing God means we:

1. See who we are.
2. See who God is.
3. Believe what God had done, is doing, and will do.
4. Respond in obedience to Him.

Let's look at this alongside King Solomon's aforementioned
command found in Proverbs 4:23, 25–27. Steps 1–3 of our definition of fearing the Lord all deal with the internal—our hearts,
which we are to guard. We must never lose biblical sight of who
we are; who God is; and what He has done, is doing, and will do.

Maintaining a biblical perspective will enable our hearts—which determine the course of our lives—to prompt an outward biblical response of obedience. Look how Solomon describes this path of obedience, which we are to look at by fixing our eyes straight ahead. By looking straight ahead, we will walk straight and safely. It's only when we look to the right or left, and then our feet follow, that we will be following evil.

This brings us back to our life-map we received a few minutes ago:

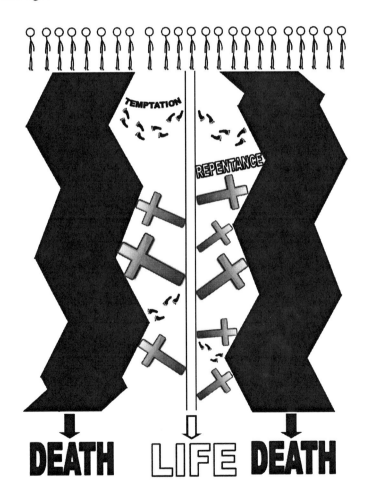

Do you see yourself at the top of the map? That's where you are at this very moment in your life. That's where you are *every* moment of your life. If you look straight ahead, you see a straight path. We already know it's a safe path, and it must be a godly path if being sidetracked means we're following evil.

The Bible tells us a lot about this straight, safe, and godly path. In fact, it's guarded and protected by God.[7] It's the path that leads upward to life,[8] the destination depicted at the bottom-center of our life-map. In addition to being straight, the path is narrow.[9] Travelers on this path understand righteousness, justice, and fairness. Guided by common sense and discernment, they find the right way to go—in other words, they continue walking straight—because their hearts are full wisdom, and knowledge fills them with joy.[10] In fact, by traveling alongside other like-minded people, those walking on the wise path to life become even wiser, and all know where they are going.[11] Carefully considering each step in prudence, those on the path are cautious to avoid evil.[12] To them, it's like an open highway![13] The path is beautiful, like the first

---

[7]   Proverbs 2:7–8 (ESV): he [God] stores up sound wisdom for the upright; he is a shield to those who walk in integrity, [8] guarding the paths of justice and watching over the way of his saints.

[8]   Proverbs 12:28 (ESV): In the path of righteousness is life, and in its pathway there is no death.
Proverbs 15:24: The path of life leads upward for the wise; they leave the grave behind.

[9]   Matthew 7:14a (ESV): For the gate is narrow and the way is hard that leads to life,

[10]   Proverbs 2:9–11 (ESV): Then you will understand righteousness and justice and equity, every good path; [10] for wisdom will come into your heart, and knowledge will be pleasant to your soul; [11] discretion will watch over you, understanding will guard you,

[11]   Proverbs 13:20a (ESV): Whoever walks with the wise becomes wise,

[12]   Proverbs 14:8a (ESV): The wisdom of the prudent is to discern his way,
Proverbs 14:15b (ESV): but the prudent gives thought to his steps.
Proverbs 14:16a (ESV): One who is wise is cautious and turns away from evil,

[13]   Proverbs 15:19b: but the path of the upright is an open highway.

beautiful rays of light piercing the fading darkness of night and continuing to shine brighter and brighter.[14]

Trailblazed by Jesus, this radical path of life is where the first becomes last. This radical path is where the ways of this world fall to the ways of Heaven. This radical path is God's kingdom on earth, only a foretaste of the perfect beauty to come in eternity. This radical path speaks of beautiful attitudes and actions for those on earth, but points to God in Heaven. This radical path, as Jesus describes in his oft-read and studied "Sermon on the Mount," which includes the "beatitudes," flips previously held customs and beliefs.

Recorded in the fifth through seventh chapters of Matthew's gospel record of Jesus' ministry, His "Sermon on the Mount" illustrates the characteristics of living with a high Spiritual Fear Factor. He taught with real, never-before-seen authority about our thoughts, attitudes, beliefs, and resulting actions, leaving listeners then—and those living with a high Spiritual Fear Factor today— amazed.[15] Summarizing Jesus' main points about those living with a high Spiritual Fear Factor, those walking on this radical path, He calls them blessed when they are:

- Believing in their need for God. This human characteristic points to God's character. God provides for us in ways that are infinitely greater than we can understand. (Matthew 5:3)
- Grieving, pointing to God's comfort for us. (5:4)
- Humble, pointing to God's sovereignty. (5:5)
- Desirous of justice, pointing to God's fair judgment. (5:6)
- Merciful, pointing to God's mercy shown first to us. (5:7)
- Pure in heart, pointing to God's intrinsic purity. (5:8)
- Making peace, pointing to God's gift of peace He gives to followers of Jesus. (5:9)

---

[14] Proverbs 4:18: The way of the righteous is like the first gleam of dawn, which shines ever brighter until the full light of day.

[15] Matthew 7:28–29 (ESV): And when Jesus finished these sayings, the crowds were astonished at his teaching, [29] for he was teaching them as one who had authority, and not as their scribes.

- Persecuted by the world, pointing to God's love for us and calling us as His followers. (5:10–12)
- Doing good deeds, pointing to God's enabling grace and greatest works that place Him as the only One worthy to be praised. (5:13–16)
- Obeying God's laws, pointing to God's perfect character. (5:17–20)
- Patient with others, pointing to God's patience with us. (5:21–22)
- Reconciling with others, pointing to God's reconciliation of mankind to Him. (5:23–26)
- Wholly devoted to Him, pointing to God's jealousy and zeal for us in perfect marriage. (5:27–32)
- Not making vows, pointing to God's ability alone to keep His covenant with us without wavering. (5:33–37)
- Generous, pointing to God's outpouring of generosity on humanity. (5:38–42)
- Loving enemies and praying for those who are persecuting them, pointing to God's love for us when we were His enemies and persecuting Him. (5:43–48)
- Giving without fanfare, pointing to God's ownership of all as the Giver of all good and perfect gifts. (6:1–4)
- Praying privately and recognizing their need for Him, pointing to God's desire for an intimate one-on-one relationship with every one of us. (6:5–13)
- Forgiving, pointing to God first forgiving us. (6:14–15)
- Fasting secretly, pointing to God's sustaining Word for our lives. (6:16–18)
- Not looking for earthly treasures, pointing to God's infinitely eternal, heavenly gifts that are worth infinitely more. (6:19–24)
- Not worrying, pointing to God's omnipotent knowledge of our needs and His perfect provisions. (6:25–34)
- Seeking the Kingdom of God first, pointing to God's pre-eminence over all other kingdoms. (6:33)
- Not judging others, pointing to God's position as the perfect Judge over all. (7:1–6)

- Seeking and knocking, pointing to God's perfect responses. (7:7–11)
- Placing others before themselves, pointing to God's Son coming to serve and give His life for us. (7:12)
- Finding and walking in the narrow, difficult gateway to life, pointing to God's Son, Jesus, being the only way to God the Father and eternal life. (7:13–14)
- Bearing good fruit in their actions, pointing to God's perfect fruit arising from His perfect character. (7:15–20)
- Doing the will of God, pointing to God's position as Lord, Master, and Commander. (7:21–23)
- Living wisely, pointing to God's immutability, His unchanging character, and that He is the Solid Rock on which we stand and live for Him. (7:24–27)

Jesus blazes the trail whose travelers are people of character, not compromise. Those are people with a high Spiritual Fear Factor, such as Enoch, who walks so closely with God that God snatches him up to Heaven. It includes people like Noah, who keeps building and building a huge boat for years in preparation for a flood before it ever rained once. People like Abraham, who does not know where he is going and is about to sacrifice His son, all because of His faith in and obedience to God. People like Joseph, who knows God can turn people's evil intentions into good. People like Moses, who commands the Israelites to sprinkle blood on their doorposts at the first Passover and then leads Israel through the Red Sea. People like a young David, who with five stones and sling-shot in hand, literally faces and defeats a giant. People like Daniel, who trusts God in a lion's den. People like Hananiah, Mishael, and Azariah,[16] who walk into a fiery furnace without fearing man, instead fearing God so much that they know God *can* save them and, whether He chooses to or not, He is the only One worthy to be worshiped. People like Hosea, who marries and then chooses to buy back and redeem an unfaithful prostitute to paint a picture of God's limitless love for Israel and for us. People like the disciples

---

[16] These are the Hebrew names of Daniel's friends. You most likely know them by their Babylonian names: Shadrach, Meshach, and Abednego.

and apostles, who count it a joy to be persecuted and ultimately die out of an unwavering fear of the Lord, when fearing man is the only way to save their earthly lives.

They are people like Martin Luther who echo the Apostle Paul's words in Philippians 1:21: "For to me, living means living for Christ, and dying is even better." Look at the following insight into Luther's life:

> Many people have commented on the fact that in Luther's first hearing before the Emperor Charles V . . . he was visibly overwhelmed. . . . [W]hat overpowered Luther was "not so much that he stood in the presence of the emperor as this, that he and the emperor alike were called upon to answer before Almighty God." Called as he had been, Luther feared God more than he feared the emperor. That is why he could say the next day [again standing before the Emperor], "My conscience is captive to the Word of God. I cannot and I will not recant anything, for to go against conscience is neither right nor safe. God help me. Amen."

Only when we join Luther standing with absolute resolve in the fear of God—and not in the fear of man—will our world be transformed. No doubt, from a human perspective it's a difficult, seemingly impossible path to walk. But, nothing is too difficult for the Lord. That's why Jesus blazed the trail for us to follow. With God, nothing is impossible! God loves those walking on this path and faithfully pours out His unfailing love upon them.[17] What a wonderful path! The path can't get any better because the only thing better is its destination—Heaven!

---

[17] Proverbs 15:9b: but he [the LORD] loves those who pursue godliness.
Proverbs 14:22b: if you plan to do good, you will receive unfailing love and faithfulness.

<3

Can a "digital native"—a person like me who has grown up living in a technological world—be considered "old school" when it comes to technology? For instance, I remember Twitter before it existed. A time with screennames as long as you wanted instead of handles less than fifteen characters. Instead of tweeting in 140 characters or less to let friends know where you were or what you were doing, you experienced the freedom of character-limitlessness by posting what was then called an "away message."[18] I also remember a time before emojis existed, when people only used emoticons.[19] Emoticons only used existing math symbols, language characters, and other marks commonly found on a keyboard to communicate or express emotional tones. Emoticons—and now emojis—attempt to fill the digital gap of nonverbal cues that are lost when communicating digitally.

Take a look at this section's heading. It's an emoticon comprised of the math symbol for "less than" and the Arabic numeral three. When put together, it's a heart. Nothing fluttered the hearts of teenagers from the mid-1990s through the early-2000s more than this two-part emoticon, a heart that could easily be chock full of the connotation of love. If you got one of those in an instant message conversation,[20] go ahead and start planning the wedding, baby!

I still use emoticons, including "<3" today. Call me old school. Or, better yet, ask, "What in the world does this have to do with fearing the Lord?" Or, *even better*, ask, "How in the world did this guy's book get published with stuff like this?"

---

[18] At this point, if you are completely lost, you are most likely older than me and a digital immigrant. You were born before technology became a ubiquitous part of the Western world. If you are only halfway lost, you are most likely younger than me and have no idea why the "save" button is a square with a couple smaller squares inside it. FYI, that's what a 3.5" disk looked like. We used to have to save files on it. Hence, it's the save button.

[19]

[20] Think of it like texting on computers before texting on cell phones existed.

If this is your question, I'm glad you asked! The answer is found in seven proverbs, or sayings of the biblically wise, which follow:

1. The LORD is watching everywhere, keeping his eye on both the evil and the good. (Proverbs 15:3)
2. For the LORD sees clearly what a man does, examining every path he takes. (Proverbs 5:21)
3. People may be right in their own eyes, but the LORD examines their heart. (Proverbs 21:2)
4. People may be pure in their own eyes, but the LORD examines their motives. (Proverbs 16:2)
5. The LORD's light penetrates the human spirit, exposing every hidden motive. (Proverbs 20:27)
6. Fire tests the purity of silver and gold, but the LORD tests the heart. (Proverbs 17:3)
7. Even Death and Destruction hold no secrets from the LORD. How much more does he know the human heart! (Proverbs 15:11)

Let's build on these seven proverbs step-by-step. First, God is watching everywhere. Second, not only is He watching, but He sees everyone and their actions clearly. He examines everyone's paths. It's not a passive, fly-by gaze, either. Nobody can hide from Him. Third, we may think we're right, but God's thorough examination may reveal otherwise. It's such a thorough examination that, fourth, our self-deception is repeated for effect. Above all, our heart is deceitful; only God knows its true condition.[21] God knows our hearts' true condition because, fifth, His light penetrates and exposes all our motives—even those hidden to others and to us. Nothing is held back. God knows His creation—you and me—intimately. This penetrating light, sixth, is part of God's thorough examination to scrutinize our innermost being—our <3 (heart). Finally, if Satan and death are laid bare before God—while yet mysterious to us—how can we not think all the above is true?

---

[21] Jeremiah 17:9 (ESV): The heart is deceitful above all things, and desperately sick; who can understand it?

God knows everything about everyone. That's part of His character. After all, He is the Creator and Sustainer of the heavens and the earth. When we see God in this (or should I say in His) light, we again gain greater understanding into who He is, and our fear of God increases.

The Crooked and Wide

At this point, God is opening our eyes at the nature preserve. We understand we have countless choices each day that are ultimately born out of the very core of our being, our spiritual heart. These choices result in us walking on certain paths in life. We recognize God, in His infinite wisdom, not only knows but examines our motivations and choices. Choosing the straight and narrow path, we can spiritually walk in wisdom by fearing God. It's this path that shines brightly with spiritual safety and blessings, leading to life.

But what about the other two paths on the map? The ones to the right and left of the path to life. Remember King Solomon's admonition in Proverbs 4:27: "Don't get sidetracked; keep your feet from following evil." Flanking the godly path are the paths of evil. As you can imagine, the biblical descriptions of these paths starkly contrast with that of the godly. The evil paths are dark and twisted, made crooked by those walking on the path who actually *enjoy* doing wrong.[22] They *despise* God.[23] Without sense, they enjoy foolishness.[24] Reckless confidence and carelessness marks them.[25]

---

[22] Proverbs 2:12–15 (ESV) says discretion and understanding (i.e., wisdom) will be "delivering you from the way of evil, from men of perverted speech, [13] who forsake the paths of uprightness to walk in the ways of darkness, [14] who rejoice in doing evil and delight in the perverseness of evil, [15] men whose paths are crooked, and who are devious in their ways."

[23] Proverbs 14:2b: those who take the wrong path despise him [the LORD].

[24] Proverbs 15:21a: Foolishness brings joy to those with no sense;

[25] Proverbs 14:16b (ESV): but a fool is reckless and careless.

So consumed with themselves, pride marks them.[26] Stubbornness marks them.[27] Evil on the inside springs forth evil on the outside.

The path is treacherous and thorny.[28] It's so dark, travelers do not even realize what makes them trip and fall.[29] For example, immoral adulterers stagger on the crooked trails on their way to the paths' destination: eternal spiritual death.[30] Ensnared by their sins, travelers on the crooked paths continue to walk in sin toward death because of their own foolishness and lack of self-control.[31] Their sins pierce them.[32] In addition to piercing, their sins crush them.[33] Sins that will ultimately be exposed.[34]

Why would anyone want to travel on these trails? We see some are ignorant, not even realizing they are on the path. We see some who *know* better, but the false allure and appearance of how they will *feel* causes them to stumble.

---

[26] Proverbs 21:4: Haughty eyes, a proud heart, and evil actions are all sin.

[27] Proverbs 28:14b: but the stubborn are headed for serious trouble.

[28] Proverbs 22:5a (ESV): Thorns and snares are in the way of the crooked;

[29] Proverbs 4:19 (ESV): The way of the wicked is like deep darkness; they do not know over what they stumble.

[30] Proverbs 5:3–6: For the lips of an immoral woman are as sweet as honey, and her mouth is smoother than oil. 4 But in the end she is as bitter as poison, as dangerous as a double-edged sword. 5 Her feet go down to death; her steps lead straight to the grave. 6 For she cares nothing about the path to life. She staggers down a crooked trail and doesn't realize it.
Proverbs 11:19b (ESV): but he who pursues evil will die.

[31] Proverbs 5:22–23 (ESV): The iniquities of the wicked ensnare him, and he is held fast in the cords of his sin. 23 He dies for lack of discipline, and because of his great folly he is led astray.

[32] Proverbs 15:19a (ESV): The way of a sluggard is like a hedge of thorns,

[33] Proverbs 11:5b: the wicked fall beneath their load of sin.

[34] Proverbs 10:9b (ESV): but he who makes his ways crooked will be found out.

From the Straight and Narrow to the Crooked and Wide

Those who have not yet heard the gospel of Jesus Christ walk ignorantly on the road that leads to death. Hence, it's incumbent for Christians to reach out and share the Good News of Jesus Christ—to show them who they are; who God is; and what God has done, is doing, and will do. Paul speaks to this in his letter to the early church in Rome:

> But how can they call on him to save them unless they believe in him? And how can they believe in him if they have never heard about him? And how can they hear about him unless someone tells them? [15] And how will anyone go and tell them without being sent? That is why the Scriptures say, "How beautiful are the feet of messengers who bring good news!" (Romans 10:14–15)

After hearing the gospel message, the ignorant are now knowledgeable. Ignorance is no longer an excuse. They find themselves standing at the most important crossroad of their life. People may stand at this crossroad, looking for only a second or for days, months, years, and decades.[35] But what about you, "follower of Jesus?" You "prayed the prayer." You "walked down the aisle to the altar." Perhaps you even remember the date. You point to it, wrongly thinking it now doesn't matter what you do; you have your "Get-Out-Of-Hell-Free Card." King Solomon warns you, "follower of Jesus," in Proverbs 1:32: "For simpletons turn away from me—to death. Fools are destroyed by their own complacency."

---

[35] The point here is not meant to divide Christians by igniting a debate on Calvinism. Personally, as we—in our limited capacity as humans on this side of eternity—live day to day, we experientially process and react to information and accordingly make choices. However, God—who we agree is all-knowing—already knows what we will decide. It is God that draws us to Himself, as Jesus says in John 6:44: "For no one can come to me unless the Father who sent me draws them to me, and at the last day I will raise them up."

The Hebrew word translated "complacency" means thinking you are spiritually prosperous and at ease because of that one moment in time. God desires a *relationship* with you—not just a *first date*. Is God speaking to you right now? Is the Holy Spirit pressing you as you think about your actions (what the Bible calls your "fruit") since that past moment in time? Even demons recognized Jesus as the Son of God and His authority, as we learned in language class. James warns, "You say you have faith, for you believe that there is one God. Good for you! Even the demons believe this, and they tremble in terror."[36] Did you really turn to Jesus? Who is the boss of your life? Has your heart deceived you into a spiritual life of supposed prosperity and ease? Don't continue to turn away from Him and experience eternal death in Hell.

If you read the above and the Holy Spirit affirms in your heart that Jesus is your Master and Commander, and you are being obedient to Him in your relationship with Him, you are eternally secure through the blood of Jesus Christ. In the big picture, you walk on the straight and narrow path leading upwardly to eternal life. Does that make you think (with pride, may I add) you are never on the wide and crooked path of evil?

Look at the biblical life-map. Do you see the multiple lines leading away from the godly path to the evil path, labeled *Temptation*? Instead of looking straight ahead, you look to the right or left. Temptation is the ever-darkening bridge leading from the godly path back down to the evil path. From the outside, temptation looks alluring and enticing, even safe. Think about Adam and Eve before they sinned. Think about you when you are tempted. When inside, meditating on temptation is arduous, evil, and even deadly. We see what happens after we are enticed and give in to temptation. King Solomon warns very early in Proverbs:

> My child, if sinners entice you, turn your back on
> them! [11] They may say, "Come and join us. Let's
> hide and kill someone. Just for fun, let's ambush
> the innocent! [12] Let's swallow them alive, like the

---

[36] James 2:19

grave; let's swallow them whole, like those who go down to the pit of death. [13] Think of the great things we'll get! We'll fill our houses with all the stuff we take. [14] Come, throw in your lot with us; we'll all share the loot."

[15] My child, do not go along with them! Stay far away from their paths. [16] They rush to commit evil deeds. They hurry to commit murder. [17] If a bird sees a trap being set, it knows to stay away. [18] But these people set an ambush for themselves; they are trying to get themselves killed. (Proverbs 1:10–18)

Regardless if we admit it, we've all been there with Peter[37] in our Christian walk. The night of Jesus' arrest, Peter adamantly denies that he'll, well, deny. He is responding to Jesus' statement in Luke 22:31 that begins, "Simon, Simon, Satan has asked to sift each of you like wheat."

Jesus and the apostles use imagery that their listeners and readers could understand in the culture of that day. Two thousand years later, sometimes we do not fully grasp or appreciate its meaning because our culture and our daily routines are very different from back then. Just what is the sifting of wheat, and how do you do it? To sift wheat means to literally tear it apart to separate the wheat grain (the valuable part) from the chaff (the worthless part). Listeners and readers in Jesus' day and in the times thereafter would immediately know of the violence that marks the sifting process. You first thresh the wheat by spreading it onto a hard floor and then beat it with a wooden staff that has a short heavy stick swinging from it. After threshing, the wheat is then winnowed. You throw the now-beaten grain into the air and the lighter, worthless chaff blows away in a decent breeze. Then, all that's left is the heavier, valuable wheat grain.

---

[37] Not Peter Brady. Simon Peter. Some of my Millennial colleagues will not understand this allusion, either. That's okay. They're probably used to it by now or don't care, anyway.

The Greek form of the word "you" that Jesus speaks is plural. He is not only talking to Peter; He is also talking to us as Christians 2,000 years later. And, we can now more fully appreciate Jesus' warning. Satan wants to tear us apart and separate us from God's goodness and holiness in our lives. This removes any sense of surprise when we literally feel torn while wrestling with temptation. Jesus tells us to expect it! Look how James describes temptation:

> And remember, when you are being tempted, do not say, "God is tempting me." God is never tempted to do wrong, and he never tempts anyone else. [14] Temptation comes from our own desires, which entice us and drag us away. [15] These desires give birth to sinful actions. And when sin is allowed to grow, it gives birth to death. (James 1:13–15)

Temptation comes from our own evil desires, dragging us away in sinful actions that, if left to grow, lead us down to the wide, dark, evil paths that lead to death.

Being tempted is not a sin. Satan tempts Jesus, yet Jesus is without sin. So, what are we as followers of Jesus to do when we are tempted and about to be drug away into sin? About to be drug into the all-too-common sense of failure. The all-too-common shame. Disappointment. Loneliness. Unworthiness. Guilt. Do you wonder if you'll ever be able to face a specific temptation and it not end in the same way, with the same feelings? You can!

The Apostle Paul describes the escape hatch we can all run to in the midst of temptation in 1 Corinthians 10:13.[38] First, he wants you to know that you're not alone or unique in your struggle. There's another Christian waging war on the same front line as you. You probably even know the person without realizing it. Moreover, God won't allow the temptation to be more than we can bear; He

---

[38] 1 Corinthians 10:13 (ESV): No temptation has overtaken you that is not common to man. God is faithful, and he will not let you be tempted beyond your ability, but with the temptation he will also provide the way of escape, that you may be able to endure it.

provides a way for us to pass the test, to win the battle. Pause and think about that for a moment. Let it soak in. *God gives us a way out!* We may feel like the walls are closing in all around us, but we can open up the hatch and escape before we become trapped. We'll see the escape hatch if we consciously look for it in God's Word and through the Holy Spirit!

For example, do you remember a time when you were facing a situation that was new to you, and you didn't know what to expect? Where did you turn? We're often comforted and reassured after listening to someone who has already gone through what we're about to experience—whether it's going to college, becoming a parent for the first time, or enduring a particular surgery. We are more at ease after understanding they were in the same situation and are still here to give us expectations and advice empathetically. In cases of temptation, we can turn to Jesus. Anything you or I have been or will be tempted with, so has Jesus. And, He never sinned. On top of that, when we're tempted, our perfect and holy Savior is at the Father's right hand interceding for us at the throne of grace. Through faith in Jesus, we can receive God's mercy and grace.[39]

God's Word implodes the bridge of temptation. Jesus—the Word made flesh, full of grace and truth[40]—and the Bible[41] will keep us from traversing temptation's downward bridge onto the crooked and wide path of sin.

---

[39] Hebrews 4:14–16 (ESV): Since then we have a great high priest who has passed through the heavens, Jesus, the Son of God, let us hold fast our confession. [15] For we do not have a high priest who is unable to sympathize with our weaknesses, but one who in every respect has been tempted as we are, yet without sin. [16] Let us then with confidence draw near to the throne of grace, that we may receive mercy and find grace to help in time of need.

[40] John 1:14 (ESV): And the Word became flesh and dwelt among us, and we have seen his glory, glory as of the only Son from the Father, full of grace and truth.

[41] Psalm 119:11 (ESV): I have stored up your word in my heart, that I might not sin against you.

From the Crooked and Wide to the Straight and Narrow

Unless you're Jesus,[42] you've crossed temptation's bridge into sin. I have crossed more than I can count or even know or can imagine. Seeing who we truly are is the first step to fearing the Lord. The Apostle John writes in 1 John 1:8, "If we claim we have no sin, we are only fooling ourselves and not living in the truth." He soon adds in 1 John 1:10, "If we claim we have not sinned, we are calling God a liar and showing that his word has no place in our hearts." This means we find ourselves on the crooked and wide path. How do we traverse from that trail to the straight and narrow, godly trail? Repentance is the bridge leading upward from the evil path to the godly path. In a sense, the act of repentance is the antithesis of acting on temptation.

Temptation, when given in to, lures us downwardly toward sinfulness. Repentance, when enacted, draws us upwardly toward holiness. Temptation feigns temporal pleasure. Repentance ensures spiritual joy. Temptation offers the opportunity for our Spiritual Fear Factor to decrease. Repentance guarantees our Spiritual Fear Factor will increase. Jesus destroys the bridge of sin after temptation. Jesus builds the bridge of repentance.

Repentance, which literally means "to turn," occurs when we confess our sins and ask God for forgiveness. Tucked between John's two quotes at the beginning of this section is the essence of Christian hope and joy is found in 1 John 1:9: "But if we confess our sins to him, he is faithful and just to forgive us our sins and to cleanse us from all wickedness." *Forgiven! Cleansed!* Free from failure, shame, disappointment, loneliness, and unworthiness!

God, speaking through the prophet Isaiah as recorded in Isaiah 44:22, says, "I have swept away your sins like a cloud. I have scattered your offenses like the morning mist. Oh, return to me, for I have paid the price to set you free." Our life-map shows more bridges of repentance than temptation that leads to sin. This symbolically represents God, in His grace and mercy, giving us an

---

[42] You're not.

infinite amount of opportunities to walk the bridge of repentance, to walk from dark into light, to rise above the morning mist and dark clouds, and to walk to a greater intimacy with Him through Jesus. Regardless of what we've done, the bridge of repentance is in the shape of a cross and colored red, painted with Jesus' blood, all so you and I can walk on it!

Keep Going

We can't just talk the talk because God knows we would be lying, which means we are sinning more. We must walk the walk. King Solomon bluntly writes in Ecclesiastes 5:7, "Talk is cheap . . . Fear God instead."

One of my former pastors, whom I also had the privilege to serve alongside, signed the closing of every email, letter, and note with the simple phrase "Keep going." Regardless of the path you are on now, keep going. If you're on the straight and narrow, keep going on it, fixing your eyes straight ahead to avoid going left or right on the bridge of temptation. If you're on the dark and twisted road, keep going to the bridge of repentance toward the godly path. Keep going amidst the pain. Keep going amidst the struggle. Keep going amidst the suffering. Keep going with hope. Keep going with Jesus and the Holy Spirit. Keep going in the fear of the Lord. The Apostle Paul tells us to keep going:

> And we believers also groan, even though we have the Holy Spirit within us as a foretaste of future glory, for we long for our bodies to be released from sin and suffering. We, too, wait with eager hope for the day when God will give us our full rights as his adopted children, including the new bodies he has promised us. (Romans 8:23)

Jesus saves us so we can keep going. So we can keep going *in the fear of God*!

Your James 1:22 Challenge

James writes to us, "But don't just listen to God's word. You must do what it says. Otherwise, you are only fooling yourselves." Use the following five prompts to apply lessons learned from this chapter centered on God's Word to transform your life.

1. What's the difference between justification and sanctification? Are you justified? Are you being sanctified?

2. Look back over the past twenty-four hours. Have you spent more time on the straight and narrow path or on the wide and crooked? How many times have you walked down the bridge of temptation? How many times have you walked up the bridge of repentance?

3. What are three areas you struggle with temptation the most? Confess these areas to a Christian brother or sister who is your accountability partner. If you don't have an accountability partner, speak with a pastor or a Christian friend who can help set up an accountability relationship for you. It's that important!

4. Do you find confessing your sins and asking for repentance to be easy, hard, or neither? Are your "confessionals" to God rudimentary, half-hearted prayers? Ask God to open your eyes to see sin as He sees it, and notice how your prayers of confession change.

5. Do you talk about fearing God and not actually live marked by it? Remember, talk is cheap; fear God instead.

Chapter 10: Surrendering Your Stone

"For most of my life, I believed that my father had broken many of my bones. They were emotional and psychological bones; things no one could see, things that caused me to limp through life clutching for and holding on to people and situations that often rendered me immobile."

- Iyanla Vanzant, American inspirational speaker, lawyer, author, and television personality

"The greatest legacy one can pass on to one's children and grand-children is not money or other material things accumulated in one's life, but rather a legacy of character and faith."

- Billy Graham, American Christian evangelist

A t this point in our journey as we walk out of the nature pre-serve, I can see the tired looks on your faces. You're ready to hop back on the bus to end the day. *Watch out!* You're so tired that you almost ran into a big mound of stones piled up in front of the bus door. *Say what?* You're wondering what's going on— *again.* The only way we can board the bus is if we all grab one of the stones. Each is uniquely shaped and patterned in ways only God can create. Each is about the size of your hand. All are heavy enough to hurt someone if you throw it at them. *Go ahead, pick up a stone.*

With your stone in hand, I now want you to imagine the strang-est-looking house you've ever seen. Picture it in your mind. What makes it look strange? Is it the shape? Its colors? Does it look out of place in its surroundings? Is it like one of those attractions where the house is literally tilted and upside down? Picture a very strange house.

Now, come back in time with me to New York City in the year 1882. We're staring at what is known the Richardson "Spite House." The house is 104 feet long, extending along Lexington Avenue, but it is only five feet wide! Yes, five feet! Less than two yards! Most of us are taller than it is wide! If we lay down on the sidewalk, we eclipse the house's width! Talk about strange! *Why in the world was this house built?* Well, a gentleman named Hyman Sarner owns several lots on East 82nd Street, and he wants to build an apartment building on his property, which extends to within a few feet of Lexington Avenue. On the Lexington Avenue side is a very long and very narrow strip of land, which he thinks is absolutely valueless for any building purpose, unless it's used in conjunction with his adjoining land. A man named Joseph Richardson owns this small, narrow piece of land that stands between Sarner's property and Lexington Avenue.

Sarner decides to offer Richardson $1,000 for the land, but Richardson flatly denies the offer, saying that he feels the property is worth very much more. Richardson makes a counter offer of $5,000. To put this in perspective, Sarner's offer is today's equivalent of $23,500. Richardson's counteroffer is a whopping $117,500. As you can imagine, Sarner refuses the counter offer, which is met by Richardson slamming the door on him and calling him names that likely aren't fit for printing.

Despite being unable to strike a deal, Sarner goes ahead with the construction of his apartment building that includes windows overlooking the thin strip of property owned by Richardson and Lexington Avenue. When the building is done, Richardson looks up, sees the windows, and decides that he will build apartments on his own narrow strip of land to block the view of Lexington Avenue from Sarner's apartments. Richardson wants Sarner to rue not paying him $5,000.

While Richardson's own family begs him not to build the house, he decides that he is not only going to build it, but he's going to live in it and rent it out, too!

Within the year, the Richardson "Spite House" (as it is now known throughout the city) is finished, and it blocks out the light from all the side windows on Sarner's property, making Richardson a happy man. The "Spite House" stands four stories tall and is divided into eight suites, two on each floor. Each suite consists of three rooms and bath, running along the Lexington Avenue side of the structure.

Only the very smallest furniture can fit into the rooms. The stairways are so narrow that only one person can use the stairs at a time. If you're a tenant and you want to go up or down from one floor to another, you have to be sure nobody else is using the stairs. The halls throughout the house are so narrow that one person can pass another only by ducking into one of the rooms until the other passes. The largest dining table in any of the suites is eighteen inches wide—less than two feet. The chairs, well, let's just say they're proportionately small.[1]

Richardson lives in the house for fifteen years. For fifteen years, he holds onto one thing—revenge for $4,000—that literally imprisons him for his life. A life marked by pride, ensnared by the fear of man, specifically the fear of self. It's amazing what we do and hold onto. While it may not show up in a "Spite House," it rears its ugliness in other spiritual areas of our lives, from our anger to our finances to our lust and to our judgment. All these can imprison us, robbing us from an abundant, free life. A life marked by the fear of the Lord.

With your stone still in hand, allow me to recount a familiar biblical account of a woman caught in adultery brought before Jesus by the Pharisees. God will speak to us about His grace, freeing us from what's holding us captive and holding down our Spiritual Fear Factor.

> Jesus returned to the Mount of Olives, [2] but early
> the next morning he was back again at the Temple.
> A crowd soon gathered, and he sat down and

---

[1] But you can at least be in the 1882 *Guinness Book of World Records* for having the smallest kitchen stove! I mean, a world record is a world record! Even in the late 1800s.

taught them. [3] As he was speaking, the teachers of religious law and the Pharisees brought a woman who had been caught in the act of adultery. They put her in front of the crowd.

[4] "Teacher," they said to Jesus, "this woman was caught in the act of adultery. [5] The law of Moses says to stone her. What do you say?"

[6] They were trying to trap him into saying something they could use against him, but Jesus stooped down and wrote in the dust with his finger. [7] They kept demanding an answer, so he stood up again and said, "All right, but let the one who has never sinned throw the first stone!" [8] Then he stooped down again and wrote in the dust.

[9] When the accusers heard this, they slipped away one by one, beginning with the oldest, until only Jesus was left in the middle of the crowd with the woman. [10] Then Jesus stood up again and said to the woman, "Where are your accusers? Didn't even one of them condemn you?"

[11] "No, Lord," she said.

And Jesus said, "Neither do I. Go and sin no more." (John 8:1–11)

Together, stones in hand, we're going to dig and find five "news" in this account. The "news" represent the facts of the event. Within those five "news," we're going to discover six steps to a new life in Christ. It's in these six application points that we can be released from what is limiting us just as Richardson's "Spite House" limited him in so many ways. Thus, we can live with a higher Spiritual Fear Factor.

A New Day

When we're familiar with something, we can miss its finer details. Accordingly, we can easily gloss right over the first two verses of this familiar encounter. God, through divine inspiration, meant for each verse and each detail to be in the Bible, including these verses. The key is between the first two verses and is our first "new": A new day.

After teaching in the Temple during the seven-day Jewish Festival of Shelters where He is ridiculed, called demon-possessed, and almost arrested, what does Jesus do the next day according to these verses? Marked not by the fear of man but by the fear of God, He goes to His favorite solitary prayer spot on the Mount of Olives to pray, and then gets up and goes back to His ministry of teaching. A new day dawns between the first two verses.

Sometimes, especially when we're in the midst of life's storms, simply getting up out of bed to start the day is the hardest thing to do. That's Step #1 in our process: *Get up.*

I remember the cold 1940s-colored pink and blue floor tiles. The kind that are about one centimeter square, requiring hundreds to cover a regularly sized bathroom. They were cold as I sat on them, frozen—not just physically, but mentally, emotionally, and spiritually. After getting out of bed when the alarm clock sounded, all I could do was will myself to muster enough energy to make it to the checkerboard of cold tiles. Satan and the world was winning. My Spiritual Fear Factor was low. Very low. If it weren't for the blessing of my wife, Kelly,[2] and her words of wisdom, I don't know how long I would've sat stoically and empty on that cold floor.

King Solomon writes in Ecclesiastes 11:7 that it is "pleasant" and "sweet" to see the light of the sun and a new day. Is a new day—whether it's the sunlight of dawn or the sounds of your digital alarm clock—pleasant to you? Is your initial thought every day a positive one? Are you thankful and excited to get up? Are you like Lady Wisdom, who laughs without fear at the future, including the

---

[2] I love you, Wifey!

upcoming day?[3] You can laugh without fear at the future only by living with a high Spiritual Fear Factor.

Jeremiah writes that God's compassions for us—in His love for us—are new every morning.[4] I wasn't excited or thinking about God's compassions for me the morning I was sitting on my bathroom floor. By that time, I hadn't been smiling at the future or seen the days as pleasant for many weeks. My Spiritual Fear Factor was as low as the floor's temperature. However, God spoke into my heart through Kelly, so I was able to get up off the floor and move forward. As I rose, so did my Spiritual Fear Factor.

Each day not only brings a new opportunity to *get up*, it brings the opportunity then to *look up* in prayer. That's Step #2: *Look up*. First we have to *get up*, and second we have to *look up*. Looking up, spiritually speaking, means seeing God's light each day, even in the midst of life's darkest storms. It means talking to Him in prayer. Looking up means our Spiritual Fear Factor is going up because looking up enables us to gain a proper perspective. It allows us to see who we are; who God is; and what God has done, is doing, and will do. It allows us to feel God's love; see His holiness, perfection, and righteousness; know He goes behind and before us;[5] and to be encouraged that in all things He works for the good of those who love Him and are called according to His purpose.[6]

Think about early explorers and travelers. Their life depended on their navigation skills, and the foundation of their guidance was built on looking up to the stars. If they didn't look up, they would be without any bearings for their journey. Just as the Wise Men

---

[3]   Proverbs 31:25: She [Lady Wisdom] is clothed with strength and dignity, and she laughs without fear of the future.

[4]   Lamentations 3:22–23 (ESV): The steadfast love of the LORD never ceases; his mercies never come to an end; [23] they are new every morning; great is your faithfulness.

[5]   Psalm 139:5a: You [The LORD] go before me and follow me.

[6]   Romans 8:28 (ESV): And we know that for those who love God all things work together for good, for those who are called according to his purpose.

looked up to a bright light in the sky given to them by God,[7] we are to look up to God, who is light,[8] in what He has given to us through prayer in the Holy Spirit.

If we *get up* and we *look up*, we are following Jesus' example. Luke's inspired, historical record shows this:

> Every day Jesus went to the Temple to teach, and each evening he returned to spend the night on the Mount of Olives. [38] The crowds gathered at the Temple early each morning to hear him. (Luke 21:37–38)

So, simply from two verses that we could easily pass over in our familiarity with the story, we note the first "new" and the first two steps toward a life in Christ with a higher Spiritual Fear Factor. A new day brings the opportunity for all of us to *get up* and *look up*. And, after we *look up*, we can look forward with the proper perspective.

A New Test

Have you ever had your day planned out only to have interruptions and challenges throw your plan out the window, seemingly before the day even started? As Jesus teaches the watching crowd, the Jewish leaders interrupt Him in an effort to challenge and trap Him.

Like Jesus then, we face challenges today. From the relatively small (cars cutting you off on the road) to the relatively big (a serious medical diagnosis), your vision of your life doesn't always go as planned. Take a moment and look back at your life. Think back to how you had envisioned it going. What unexpected curveballs came your way? How has life not turned out like you planned?

While I was growing up, people often pointed me toward being a lawyer or doctor. The Lord blessed my academic career through

---

[7] Matthew 2:2: "Where is the newborn king of the Jews? We [the Wise Men] saw his star as it rose, and we have come to worship him."

[8] 1 John 1:5b (ESV): God is light, and in him is no darkness at all.

college, and I earned a full ride to law school. The "signs of the time" sure seemed to indicate the path I was on was what I was supposed to be doing. However, with a low Spiritual Fear Factor, I kept stubbornly pushing through that still, small voice telling me God had a different plan. As He always does, God finally got through my stubbornness and, a week into law school, I am pretty sure I became the first kid on a full ride to withdraw. It is a gut-wrenching time when the career path you've been preparing for all your life is suddenly no longer before you. This is a personal example of a challenge that I faced. Like Jesus, you and I are challenged in front of others, whether it's a watching world—or a watching Lord.[9] How I responded to that change would tell others a lot about where I placed my faith.

Like Jesus, we need not be surprised when challenges come each day, which is the second of our five "news": A new test.

Let's take a look at the test before Jesus. According to the Jewish law, at least two witnesses are necessary to confirm the guilt of a person accused of a crime.[10] Being caught in the actual act of committing adultery seems highly unlikely, so the religious leaders may have deliberately planned to catch her in the act. Further, according to the law, the man is required to be brought with the woman, as both deserve to die.[11] Perhaps the man escapes, perhaps he is part of the Pharisees' trap, or perhaps the Pharisees simply don't care about justice being doled out as prescribed by the law. In essence, the Pharisees are disregarding the same law they so piously act like they follow.

The Pharisees' purpose of bringing the woman before Jesus is to discredit Him as a teacher. If Jesus condemns her to be executed, they can report him to the Roman government, which did not permit

---

[9] Proverbs 15:3: The LORD is watching everywhere, keeping his eye on both the evil and the good.

[10] Deuteronomy 19:15 (ESV): "A single witness shall not suffice against a person for any crime or for any wrong in connection with any offense that he has committed. Only on the evidence of two witnesses or of three witnesses shall a charge be established."

[11] Leviticus 20:10 (ESV): "If a man commits adultery with the wife of his neighbor, both the adulterer and the adulteress shall surely be put to death."

the Jews to carry out their own executions. Additionally, it will not align with his ministry built on grace and mercy. If Jesus does not condemn her, however, He will be violating the Jewish law of Moses. I don't know about you, but I'd say this situation qualifies as a test!

Let's put this test in perspective, though. Jesus knows why He's come to earth and, ultimately, what will happen to Him so He can fulfill His purpose from the Father. He knows the torture, the crucifixion, the separation from God His Father looming ahead— all so He can bear *our* sins to reconcile *us* to Himself. Jesus knows the ultimate challenge will be when God the Father forsakes Him, God the Son, on the cross of Calvary. He knows ahead of time, too, that this challenge will come from the Pharisees, which ultimately pales in comparison to what lies ahead.

Are you and I like Jesus? Do we expect challenges? Do we expect tests? Do we expect to suffer? That's Step #3 to a new life in Christ and living with a higher Spiritual Fear Factor: *Expect challenges*. A new day brings new tests. Each day, after we *get up* and *look up*, we know to *expect challenges*.

A New Covenant

Right now, let's take a second to envision the situation. Can you feel the tension? The crowd intently watches. The group of religious leaders impatiently demands. The woman insecurely fears. And Jesus intriguingly writes.

Like the stone you're holding in front of the bus outside the nature preserve, the stones are clenched by the hands of the Pharisees. The religious leaders are ready to throw the stones—to kill. The crowd, the Pharisees, and the woman are all staring at the face of God while fearing man. How will the hallmarks of Jesus' teaching and ministry—mercy and grace—be reconciled with the punishment prescribed in the Old Testament law? What will happen to this woman? And to Jesus?

Jesus' one sentence answer—"Let he who is without sin cast the first stone"—embodies His teachings about the law in the Sermon on the Mount:

> "Don't misunderstand why I have come. I did not
> come to abolish the law of Moses or the writ-
> ings of the prophets. No, I came to accomplish
> their purpose. [18] I tell you the truth, until heaven
> and earth disappear, not even the smallest detail
> of God's law will disappear until its purpose is
> achieved." (Matthew 5:17–18)

Jesus came to fulfill the law and accomplish its purpose, not only to bear the punishment of this woman's adultery, but also to bear the sins of those ready to stone her.

This is the third "new": A new covenant.

This new covenant not only applies to the woman caught in adultery, it also applies to us. Jesus, God in human form, came to earth to do the same for you and me as He does for her. God's law is fulfilled by God's grace in the form of Jesus Christ. Is your faith in His death and resurrection helping increase your Spiritual Fear Factor? Jesus understood His purpose. Do you understand His purpose?

Jesus' statement is significant. Because He upholds the legal penalty for adultery—stoning—He can't be accused of being against Jewish law. However, by saying that only a sinless person could throw the first stone, Jesus highlights the importance of compassion and forgiveness.

You need to know something else about me:[12] I really love going to the beach. That's where I can see God in nature the most. For some, they see God's handiwork in trees and mountains. For me, it's in the ocean waves and sea shells—countless different shapes and hues of shells all glorifying God as they're washed up onto the beach.[13] In my heart, I am worshipping God, marveling at His creation—my Spiritual Fear Factor increasing. Furthermore, I also know my wife, Kelly, loves going to the beach, and I want to do whatever I can to make her happy!

---

[12] Even if you don't want to. Sorry.

[13] For me, looking for seashells on the beach is like perusing God's free souvenir shop. Every gift is uniquely designed with brilliant, magnificent colors and shapes. And, the shop has the most stunning background in the world!

I'm sure a lot of you have been to the beach. Have you ever seen anything written in the sand by someone's finger? Perhaps it's someone declaring his love for another or drawing his favorite sports team's logo. The writing is crystal clear when first written in dry sand. But, as the ocean begins to wash over the writing, it then disappears. After the ocean waves wash over all the writing and then the tide recedes, no trace of the writing is seen.

In this often-told and -studied historical event, the waves of time wash away what Jesus writes in the sand. Many have tried to guess what Jesus wrote; however, we simply don't know. God chose not to reveal it to us in His Word. With that said, though, let's take a moment and think about what Jesus *could* be writing. Perhaps Jesus writes to remind the Pharisees that He Himself had written the Law.[14] Perhaps He writes, "Do not be a malicious witness."[15] Or, perhaps He writes out the sins of the accusers.[16]

Regardless, Jesus' response—that only one who is without sin can judge—points to the Pharisees' own sinfulness and, at the same time, to Himself as the only competent Judge because of His sinlessness. As recorded in John 8:16, Jesus says, "Yet even if I do judge, my judgment is true, for it is not I alone who judge, but I and the Father who sent me."

In 2 Corinthians 12:9 (ESV), Paul writes of how Jesus said to him, "My grace is sufficient for you, for my power is made perfect in weakness." Step #4 to a new life in Christ with a higher Spiritual Fear Factor is remembering, like Paul, to *live in grace*. The main idea of this study is God's grace as exemplified in Jesus Christ. Jesus' reaction is one full of truth and grace. Truth and

---

[14] Exodus 31:18 (ESV): And he gave to Moses, when he had finished speaking with him on Mount Sinai, the two tablets of the testimony, tablets of stone, written with the finger of God.

[15] Exodus 23:1 (ESV): "You shall not spread a false rumor. You shall not join hands with a wicked man to be a malicious witness."

[16] Jeremiah 17:13 (ESV): O LORD, the hope of Israel, all who forsake you shall be put to shame; those who turn away from you shall be written in the earth, for they have forsaken the LORD, the fountain of living water.

grace undergird the bridge of repentance we are to walk on every day—back onto the straight and narrow path.

A new day brings new challenges, but also a new covenant. Are you trying to live under the Old Testament law, or the New Testament covenant of grace through Jesus Christ? Like sand being washed over by the ocean, the Old Testament law is washed over by the blood of Jesus.

A New Response

Have you ever been listening to someone talk to a large crowd and feel like they're talking directly to you only? I'm guessing that's how the Pharisees feel after Jesus' reply.

> When the accusers heard this, they slipped away one by one, beginning with the oldest, until only Jesus was left in the middle of the crowd with the woman. (John 8:9)

Jesus' words cut to people's innermost beings—their hearts and souls. His words prompt a new response from the crowd. That's the fourth "new": A new response.

Can you hear the stones dropping? First, you hear just a few thuds as the older religious leaders of the day recognize their own sin and walk away. Soon, it's a thunder of thuds as the rest of the group drop their stones and disperse in front of the gathered crowd. Stones dropped. Intentions surrendered to an increased fear of God.

Do Jesus' words cut to you like they did to this group? The Bible tells the story of the Holy God's relentless pursuit of an unholy people. When you read and listen to God's Word, how long does it take you to drop your stone? None of us can say we haven't done wrong in front of a holy, perfect God. We've all ***POPPED!*** balloons. We've all walked on the crooked and wide path. It's this realization that changes the way we look at ourselves and others. We show mercy on others because God first showered mercy on us.[17]

---

[17] Matthew 6:14–15: "If you forgive those who sin against you, your heavenly Father will forgive you. [15] But if you refuse to forgive others, your Father will

Jesus' authoritative word strikes conviction of sin in the crowd's hearts. Matthew describes Jesus' teaching as follows:

> When Jesus had finished saying these things, the crowds were amazed at his teaching, [29] for he taught with real authority—quite unlike their teachers of religious law. (Matthew 7:28–29)

These are the same teachers of religious law who are now dropping their stones and walking away. These are the same men who are going from trying to trap to being trapped, from trying to convict to being convicted.

Living with a high Spiritual Fear Factor means we live with sense of astonishment at Jesus Christ as He's revealed in His Word by the Holy Spirit. Is your hand still clenching your stone, or are you ready to drop your stone? That's Step #5 to living a new life in Christ with a higher Spiritual Fear Factor: *Drop your stone.*

What does your stone look like? They come in all shapes and sizes. The largest stone each one of us clenches from the moment we are born is the stone of man's sin that separates us from a right relationship with the Holy God of the universe. While Jesus is saving this woman from death by stoning, He knows He will soon die on the cross, not only for this woman but for you and me.

If you've made it this far in our journey, you are probably saying in the Spirit that you've dropped that stone. Maybe you dropped it decades ago. That doesn't mean you or I aren't carrying one today. I want to reiterate that stones come in all shapes and sizes. Perhaps yours looks like anger or bitterness at God for something in your life that you think should be better. What about a judgmental attitude toward fellow Christians—those with whom you are supposed to love—or toward those who have yet to come

---

not forgive your sins." (A note: This passage often can be misinterpreted and lead people down a slippery slope to a false, works-based salvation, compared to the one and only true salvation through faith alone in Jesus. We can't earn forgiveness from God by forgiving others. Rather, Jesus speaks to the essentialness of forgiveness. Day by day, we receive mercy and forgiveness by God that, in turn, will promote us to give mercy and forgive others.)

to Christ? Maybe it looks like a particular area of sin with which you continue to struggle. Stones of anger. A seemingly unrelenting stone of lust. An ever-gnawing stone of worry. Chatty stones of gossip. Does your stone look like reoccurring guilt over a sin that you've confessed, perhaps many times, to God and asked for His forgiveness?

We are to *get up, look up, expect challenges, live in grace,* and *drop our stone.*

Because the witnesses and the accusers leave, the legal case against the woman is—how fitting is this—dropped. Stones dropped. Case dropped! And what a joy it is to know that the story is not over!

A New Life

Defined as "an occasion when nobody speaks, although people are aware that there are feelings or thoughts to express," it is more commonly known as the "pregnant pause." The Pharisees, humbled and convicted with a momentarily higher Spiritual Fear Factor, embarrassingly slither their way through the gathered crowd and are present no longer. It's easy to imagine the pregnant pause before Jesus rises and speaks.

> When the accusers heard this, they slipped away one by one, beginning with the oldest, until only Jesus was left in the middle of the crowd with the woman. [10] Then Jesus stood up again and said to the woman, "Where are your accusers? Didn't even one of them condemn you?"
>
> [11] "No, Lord," she said.
>
> And Jesus said, "Neither do I. Go and sin no more." (John 8:9–11)

Ripped out of the short-lived pleasure of a sinful act to be exposed and severely punished by religious leaders in front of a crowd, the woman most likely thinks her life is over. Yet, Jesus' words give her a new life. That's the fifth "new": A new life.

A new day, a new test, a new covenant, a new response, and a new life.

The woman leaves her encounter with Jesus reenergized and free from condemnation from God, which must have seemed impossible only seconds before. Think about it and try to imagine: She is set free! A chance to begin anew! In eight words, Jesus frees her from the fear of man to live freely in the fear of the Lord! The Apostle Paul phrases the truth this way in Romans 8:1–2: "So now there is no condemnation for those who belong to Christ Jesus. And because you belong to him, the power of the life-giving Spirit has freed you from the power of sin that leads to death." In Jesus, we share this freedom from condemnation and, in the Holy Spirit, we walk free from sin's grip on our lives. We can walk on the straight and narrow path. We can return to it on the bridge of repentance.

When was the last time you encountered Jesus face-to-face? Confess your sins and walk free! That's Step #6 in our mini-study learning how to live a new life in Christ with a higher Spiritual Fear Factor: *Be free*. The Apostle John proclaims in John 8:36, "So if the Son sets you free, you are truly free." Praise God!

Jesus' words reveal Him as the Master Teacher. He rebukes sin but at the same time gives the woman hope for a new life. Theologically speaking, Jesus can forgive her sin because He has the authority and because He is the Lamb of God who bore the sin of the world.[18] And, He deals with her graciously as the One who is full of grace.

Being free doesn't mean we can do whatever we want; it means if we are confessing our sins and walking on the bridge of repentance, we are free from guilt. We are free from trying unsuccessfully to keep God's perfect law. We are free to live in a continual act of obedience out of God's love He first showed to us.[19] We are free to love God because He first loved us. We are free to

---

[18] John 1:29 (ESV): The next day he [John the Baptist] saw Jesus coming toward him, and said, "Behold, the Lamb of God, who takes away the sin of the world!"

[19] Hey, that's Step #4 of our definition of fearing the Lord!

love and serve one another. We are free to live an abundant life.[20] Are you free? Or, are you spiritually living in a narrow apartment where there's only barely any room for you? Before we get on the bus and head home to end our day, I'll ask you what I would ask Joseph Richardson back in 1882: *Are you ready to drop your stone and be free?*

Get up. Look up. Expect challenges. Live in grace. Drop your stone. Be free.

It's my prayer that you will drop the stone you're holding — whatever it may be. Let's glorify God by living a life marked by freedom in Christ, and with a high Spiritual Fear Factor, as He calls us to do.

Whenever you're ready, drop your stone, hop on the bus, and get ready for our capstone seminar. It's the final leg of our journey together.

Your James 1:22 Challenge

James writes to us, "But don't just listen to God's word. You must do what it says. Otherwise, you are only fooling yourselves." Use the following five prompts to apply lessons learned from this chapter centered on God's Word to transform your life.

1. Today and tomorrow, intentionally ask God to enable you to think pleasant, sweet, and good thoughts when you first wake up. Keep trying each day. Likewise, intentionally pray with God tomorrow morning. Read and meditate on a Bible passage, too. Start your day off nourishing yourself spiritually. See how your attitude throughout the day compares to days when you don't. With John 15:5 in mind,[21]

---

[20] John 10:10b (ESV): I [Jesus] came that they [followers of Him] may have life and have it abundantly.

[21] Jesus says in John 15:5 (ESV): "I am the vine; you are the branches. Whoever abides in me and I in him, he it is that bears much fruit, *for apart from me you*

let God work in you to make it a habit in your life to pray and meditate on His Word every morning.

2. Learn to expect challenges and embrace them with Romans 8:28 in your heart and mind.[22] Embrace your challenges by praying, "Lord, right now, I can't see how you are working this for my good, but I am trusting you and looking forward to seeing what you do."

3. Do you subtly think that whether you do more "good" things or more "bad" things affects how God sees you? That's a works-based, false doctrine of salvation. Live in grace, knowing God sees you clothed in Jesus' righteousness. On the other hand, are you abusing grace? Are you using it as an excuse to do whatever you want? Recognize and confess it as a sin to God if you are abusing the freedom God's grace provides.

4. Write down three stones you are clenching. Pray and ask God to help you drop them. Talk with your accountability partner, pastor, church leader, or trusted Christian friend. Share your struggles. *Christianity is a team sport!*

5. Ask God to bring to your heart and mind any spiritual stones you may be holding every time you physically see a rock or stone. If you are able to at the time, pick up the stone, hold on to it, and then drop it. May it be a reminder to drop your spiritual stones and surrender those areas of your life to God.

---

can do nothing." (emphasis added)

[22] Romans 8:28 (ESV): And we know that for those who love God all things work together for good, for those who are called according to his purpose.

Part 3:

Learning for Eternity

Chapter 11: Freed Forever from Fear

"The day which we fear as our last is but the birthday of eternity."
- Lucius Annaeus Seneca, Roman Stoic philosopher, statesman, and dramatist

"I have loved you, my people, with an everlasting love. With unfailing love I have drawn you to myself."
- The LORD, as recorded in Jeremiah 31:3

Watching my grandmother pull the mug of now-hot water out of the microwave and adding food coloring to it meant I was ready for one of my favorite childhood activities: Coloring Easter eggs. Using the special dipper with a circle at the bottom of a vertical rod and a handle at its top, we carefully created a rainbow of eggs. *That is so 20th century.*

Now, in the *modern 21st century,* many associate the term "Easter eggs" as little surprises or jokes tucked away in lines of computer coding. If you know the secret things to press or say at a certain time, you reap the benefits of something ranging from stupid to special.

As I admitted before, I may be a little "old school" for a "digital native" when it comes to technology. I used my Blackberry—you know, the one with the trackball and keys so small you always hit at least three letters at once—until I had to throw it on the floor for it to work. Yes, you read that right. I threw it on the floor so it would work. Except one day I threw it on the floor, and it didn't work anymore.[1] This led me, as a late adopter, to dive into the foray of phones with "personal assistants" who have funky names to match their funky voices.

One day while surfing the Internet,[2] I came across an Easter egg for my smartphone. Being the nerd I am, I found it pretty funny. With politeness, respect, and a hint of anticipation, I asked my personal digital assistant, "What is zero divided by zero?" Her reply:

> Imagine that you have zero cookies and you split them evenly among zero friends. How many cookies does each person get? See, it doesn't make sense. And Cookie Monster is sad that there are no cookies. And you are sad that you have no friends.

$0 \div 0 = $ Indeterminate

Once you sop up the coffee you spit out while laughing at her hilarity,[3] look at the real answer she gives after her Easter-egg-of-a-story. Zero divided by zero equals "indeterminate." In "mathspeak," "indeterminate" can be translated as "does not exist."

Remember in math class when we discussed numerators and denominators? Any fraction or equation with a denominator of zero "does not exist." Said differently, it's impossible to divide any number by zero, regardless of how big or small the number in the numerator is. Try dividing it by zero, and you get the same answer: Indeterminate. Mathematically, it does not exist.

In case your eyes and mind are now glazed over like hot fresh doughnuts,[4] I'll go ahead and rewrite the mathematical expression for our Spiritual Fear Factor:

---

[1] Can't say I didn't see that one coming . . .

[2] See the second paragraph of this book's introduction.

[3] I know you are. You *have* to be. How could you *not* be?

[4] Mmm. Doughnuts.

$$\text{Spiritual Fear Factor} = \frac{\text{Fear of God}}{\text{Fear of Man}} = \frac{\text{Fear of God}}{(\text{Fear of Others})\,(\text{Fear of Self})}$$

To calculate our Spiritual Fear Factor, the numerator is our Fear of God and denominator is the Fear of Man, which is comprised of the Fear of Others and the Fear of Self.

Keep that in mind as we read the Apostle John's words in his first letter to the early church:

> Dear friends, let us continue to love one another, for love comes from God. Anyone who loves is a child of God and knows God. [8] But anyone who does not love does not know God, for God is love.
>
> [9] God showed how much he loved us by sending his one and only Son into the world so that we might have eternal life through him. [10] This is real love—not that we loved God, but that he loved us and sent his Son as a sacrifice to take away our sins.
>
> [11] Dear friends, since God loved us that much, we surely ought to love each other. [12] No one has ever seen God. But if we love each other, God lives in us, and his love is brought to full expression in us.
>
> [13] And God has given us his Spirit as proof that we live in him and he in us. [14] Furthermore, we have seen with our own eyes and now testify that the Father sent his Son to be the Savior of the world. [15] All who declare that Jesus is the Son of God have God living in them, and they live in God. [16] We know how much God loves us, and we have put our trust in his love.
>
> God is love, and all who live in love live in God, and God lives in them. [17] *And as we live in God, our love grows more perfect. So we will not be*

afraid on the day of judgment, but we can face him with confidence because we live like Jesus here in this world.

[18] *Such love has no fear, because perfect love expels all fear. If we are afraid, it is for fear of punishment, and this shows that we have not fully experienced his perfect love.* [19] We love each other because he loved us first. (1 John 4:7–19; emphasis added)

Fear and love. How do they reconcile with one another as we live today and in eternity?

This portion of John's letter exhorts the early church and us to love one another. First, he identifies the *source* of all love—God—because one of God's inherent, unchanging qualities is that He is love. Then, John offers the *proof* of God's love, which is when He sent Jesus to pay the penalty for our sins. After proclaiming the gospel of Jesus Christ by defining real love in verse 10, John promotes our *response*—to love each other—in verses 11 and 12. Followers of Jesus are the earthly expression of God's love!

In verse 17, John speaks of sanctification, which we recently learned about in the nature preserve and the paths on which we walk. Sanctification—growing and maturing spiritually to live and love more and more like Jesus—entails being obedient to the Holy Spirit's direction to cause our eyes to be fixed on Jesus Christ and the narrow, godly path that leads to life. Then, when we act on a temptation and start to cross the bridge to sin and down to the dark, wide path, we turn and cross the bridge of repentance up to the path that leads to life. This is what John refers to when he writes "as we live in God, our love grows more perfect."

Fear first enters John's exhortation in the second half of verse 17. As a result of sanctification and our spiritual growth—living with an increasing Spiritual Fear Factor—we will not be afraid to stand before God on Judgment Day. This speaks to the absence of the *threat-fear* we learned about earlier. If we are in a right relationship with Jesus, we can confidently look forward to the blessing and joy awaiting us in eternity. John plainly says in the second part of verse 18 that he is indeed speaking of the fear of punishment: "If we are afraid, it is for fear of punishment, and this shows we have not fully experienced his perfect love."

However, take a look at the first part of verse 18: "Such love has no fear, because perfect love expels all fear." You may have heard this phrase translated "perfect love casts out all fear." John is referring to fear in eternity. There will be no fear at all in Heaven. Fear will not exist, and the equation for our Spiritual Fear Factor supports it.

In Heaven, everything will be perfect. Our bodies will be glorified.[5] We will bear God's name.[6] He will be with us. Death, pain, sorrow, grief, suffering will all be in eternity past, never to return.[7] In Heaven, we'll continually worship our God.[8] Our fear of God will be higher than the heavens, higher than we can imagine or comprehend. It will literally be infinitely high. Plugging this into our equation, we see:

---

[5] Philippians 3:21 (ESV): who [Jesus] will transform our lowly body to be like his glorious body, by the power that enables him even to subject all things to himself.

[6] Revelation 22:4: And they will see his face, and his name will be written on their foreheads.

[7] Revelation 21:3–4: I heard a loud shout from the throne, saying, "Look, God's home is now among his people! He will live with them, and they will be his people. God himself will be with them. 4 He will wipe every tear from their eyes, and there will be no more death or sorrow or crying or pain. All these things are gone forever."

[8] Revelation 5:11–14: Then I looked again, and I heard the voices of thousands and millions of angels around the throne and of the living beings and the elders. 12 And they sang in a mighty chorus: "Worthy is the Lamb who was slaughtered—to receive power and riches and wisdom and strength and honor and glory and blessing." 13 And then I heard every creature in heaven and on earth and under the earth and in the sea. They sang: "Blessing and honor and glory and power belong to the one sitting on the throne and to the Lamb forever and ever." 14 And the four living beings said, "Amen!" And the twenty-four elders fell down and worshiped the Lamb.

$$\frac{\text{Our Heavenly}}{\text{Spiritual Fear Factor}} = \frac{\text{Fear of God}}{\text{Fear of Man}} = \frac{\text{Positive Infinity}}{(\text{Fear of Others})\,(\text{Fear of Self})}$$

If "positive infinity" throws you off, simply think of it as a really big number. It could be a thousand, a million, a billion, whatever big number you want it to be.

In Heaven, all the glory goes to God. To Jesus, the Lamb who was slain. Notice what or who isn't in Heaven? With glorified bodies, we will be fervently worshipping God in a place unstained by sin. Just as it was in the Garden of Eden before the world's first terrorist attack and the Fall, there will be no fear of man. We will all be glorified and perfected by God. In glorified perfection, we can do nothing but perfectly worship God, spiritually unable to place anyone—whether it's others or ourselves—above Him. So, we now have the denominator to our equation for our heavenly Spiritual Fear Factor: Zero. Plugging that in gives us:

$$\frac{\text{Our Heavenly}}{\text{Spiritual Fear Factor}} = \frac{\text{Fear of God}}{\text{Fear of Man}} = \frac{\text{Positive Infinity}}{\text{Zero}}$$

Written another way: Our heavenly Spiritual Fear Factor equals positive infinity divided by zero ($+\infty \div 0$).

Do you recall having no cookies to share with no friends—and Cookie Monster being sad? Any number, regardless of how big it is—even numbers that are beyond our human comprehension like positive infinity—divided by zero is "indeterminate." Or, said in an alternate way: It does not exist.

$$\frac{\text{Our Heavenly}}{\text{Spiritual Fear Factor}} = \frac{\text{Fear of God}}{\text{Fear of Man}} = \frac{\text{Positive Infinity}}{\text{Zero}} = \text{Does Not Exist}$$

In Heaven, our Spiritual Fear Factor *does not exist*. Living in perfect union and love with God and His other sons and daughters in Jesus eliminates all fear. Fear doesn't exist when perfect love infinitely abounds. Hence, "perfect love casts out all fear." And with that, our journey nears its end. All that's left? Graduation!

Your James 1:22 Challenge

James writes to us, "But don't just listen to God's word. You must do what it says. Otherwise, you are only fooling yourselves." Use the following five prompts to apply lessons learned from this chapter centered on God's Word to transform your life.

1. Are you scared because of your sin as you anticipate Judgment Day, or are you confident in Christ? In other words, are you experiencing *threat-fear* or *worship-fear*?

2. On a calculator, try dividing a number by zero. See what happens.

3. What do you think Heaven will be like? Prayerfully ask God to give you as much comprehension of His glory as humanly possible. How does knowing what Heaven holds for those rightly related to God through Jesus Christ inspire you to act today?

4. What do you think about the idea of perfect love casting out fear? Do you agree with Tim's interpretation?

5. Think about to whom you can show more love in your life. Prayerfully ask God to be at work in you to love them more in both word and deed. Also, ask God to be at work through you, praying that when you show love, you will have the opportunity to talk about how God first loved us.

Commencement:
The Graduating Conclusion

The only appropriate way to end our educational journey is to have a graduation ceremony! One hallmark of most graduation ceremonies is the commencement speech. Whether you graduated five days ago or five decades ago, let me ask you a simple question: Do you remember who gave yours or what was said? If you're like me, you can't. However, I became enamored with an address given by Admiral William H. McRaven, who last served as the ninth commander of the United States Special Operations Command from August 8, 2011, to August 28, 2014. His address to the University of Texas Class of 2014 entitled "If You Want to Change the World" gives them—and us—ten life lessons to apply as we move forward in life.

We'll take these ten life lessons and add a biblical perspective to review what we've learned. At the same time, we will be encouraged to live marked by the fear of God to transform a world centered on the fear of man. What does the future hold spiritually for a world centered on the fear of man? The Pew Research Center provides two very relevant insights. First, Islam will be the fastest growing religion in the world and will likely become the world's largest religious group in the last half of the 21st century, surpassing Christianity. Second, fewer Americans will identify themselves as Christians while the number of "nones"—those who don't identify with any religion—will grow.

The crowd grows quiet after giving Admiral McRaven a standing ovation.

Lesson #1: Make Your Bed

> **Admiral McRaven:** "It was a simple task, mundane at best, but every morning, we were required to make our bed to perfection. It seemed a little ridiculous at the time, particularly in the light of the fact that we were aspiring to be real warriors—tough, battle-hardened [Navy] Seals—but the wisdom of this simple act has been proven to me many times over. . . . Making your bed will . . . reinforce the fact that the little things in life matter. If you can't do the little things right, you'll never be able to do the big things right. . . . So if you want to change the world, start off by making your bed."

Every aspect of military training is designed for a specific purpose; nothing is done "by accident" or "just for fun." Compare Admiral McRaven's conclusion with Jesus' words spoken to His disciples:

> If you are faithful in little things, you will be faithful in large ones. But if you are dishonest in little things, you won't be honest with greater responsibilities. [11] And if you are untrustworthy about worldly wealth, who will trust you with the true riches of heaven? [12] And if you are not faithful with other people's things, why should you be trusted with things of your own? (Luke 16:10–12)

All that we have on earth—from each breath to each possession—belongs to God. The days He gives us are filled with opportunities He entrusts to us to handle biblically. God also allows Satan to tempt us. Whether it's a little lie, a little road rage, a little laziness, a little moment of lust, a little missed opportunity to help, or even a little "good" deed done with impure motives, God watches and sees even the smallest things. How are you handling the little things in your life?

Living marked by the fear of God to transform a world centered on the fear of man requires stepping back from the big things in life, and, through the Holy Spirit, doing the little things right.

Lesson #2: Find Someone to Help You Paddle

> **Admiral McRaven:** "[Describing how teams of seven prospective Seals on one boat must paddle for several miles through exceedingly tough surf] For the boat to make it to its destination, everyone must paddle. You can't change the world alone; you will need some help. And to truly get from your starting point to your destination takes friends, colleagues, . . . and a strong coxswain to guide you. If you want to change the world, find someone to help you paddle."

Admiral McRaven describes how every person on the boat team must exert the exact same amount of energy at the exact same time, as yelled by the coxswain (you can think of the coxswain as the boat's captain) for the boat to reach its destination. As the body of Christ, our eternal destination awaits us in Heaven, but how are we to "paddle" today in life? First, we recognize that we have the Coxswain of coxswains, the Captain of captains—the Holy Spirit—living in us. The Holy Spirit reveals God's living and active Word that points us to be more like Jesus Christ. We are to be merciful, kind, humble, gentle, patient, forgiving, thankful, and—above all—loving.[1] Through the Holy Spirit, we clearly see in God's Word

---

[1] Colossians 3:12–15 (ESV): Put on then, as God's chosen ones, holy and beloved, compassionate hearts, kindness, humility, meekness, and patience, [13] bearing with one another and, if one has a complaint against another, forgiving each other; as the Lord has forgiven you, so you also must forgive. [14] And above all these put on love, which binds everything together in perfect harmony. [15] And let the peace of Christ rule in your hearts, to which indeed you were called in one body. And be thankful.

the straight passage He maps out for us to travel *together with one another* to earthly peace and eternal life.

Living marked by the fear of God to transform a world centered on the fear of man requires finding others to paddle through life together, being led by the Holy Spirit and holding one another accountable.

Lesson #3: Measure by Heart

Admiral McRaven: "The best boat crew we had was made up of little guys; the 'Munchkin Crew' we called them. No one was over 5'5".... They outpaddled, outran, and outswam all the other boat crews. The big men in the other boat crews would always make good-natured fun of the tiny, little flippers 'The Munchkins' put on their tiny, little feet prior to every swim. But, somehow, these little guys from every corner of the nation and the world always had the last laugh, swimming faster and reaching the shore long before the rest of us. . . . If you want to change the world, measure a person by the size of their heart, not by the size of their flippers."

In everyday life, the "flippers" Admiral McRaven refers to aren't flippers at all. In fact, life's flippers are the components of the fear of man. How do we measure and judge someone? How do we compare ourselves to others? What makes us envious of someone? A bigger house? A nicer car? Physical beauty? More Twitter followers, retweets, Facebook friends, or liked posts?

A rich, young man walked away from following Jesus because — despite keeping all the commandments — the young man's heart clung to his possessions. Afterwards, Jesus tells His disciples:

But many who are the greatest now will be least important then, and those who seem least important now will be the greatest then. (Matthew 19:30)

How do you measure by heart? How do you measure *your* heart? How do you measure others? The measurement that matters in eternity—God's only measurement—is your faith in following Jesus as your Savior and Lord—in other words, your Spiritual Fear Factor.

Living marked by the fear of God to transform a world centered on the fear of man requires understanding that God measures you by your heart and its relatedness to Jesus Christ.

Lesson #4: Keep Moving Forward

> **Admiral McRaven:** "Several times a week, the instructors would line up the class and do a uniform inspection. It was exceptionally thorough. . . . But, it seemed that no matter how much effort . . . it just wasn't good enough. The instructors would just find something wrong. . . . There were many a student who just couldn't accept the fact that all their efforts were in vain, and no matter how hard they tried to get the uniform right, it went unappreciated. Those students didn't make it through training. Those students didn't understand the purpose of the drill. You were never going to succeed. You were never going to have a perfect uniform; the instructors weren't going to allow it. . . . If you want to change the world . . . keep moving forward."

Regardless of how much we try to have a clean spiritual uniform, all human beings stand before God wearing a uniform stained with sin. Many religions or philosophies try to remove the stain by laying out rule after rule that must be followed to the letter. Even then, it still may not result in salvation. Everything is based on human effort—not God's. Christianity is the one and only religion that believes it is God who acts to save us. Salvation is given by God's grace—in other words, He gives us something we don't deserve—and by His grace alone. The Apostle Paul writes:

> God saved you by his grace when you believed.
> And you can't take credit for this; it is a gift from
> God. [9] Salvation is not a reward for the good things
> we have done, so none of us can boast about it. [10]
> For we are God's masterpiece. He has created us
> anew in Christ Jesus, so we can do the good things
> he planned for us long ago. (Ephesians 2:8–10)

Note in verse 10 one of the reasons God creates us anew: To
do the good things He planned for us long ago. Believing and
receiving God's gift of grace is just the beginning of a new abundant life full of good works to glorify Him—a life marked with
the clean clothes of Jesus' righteousness and by a high Spiritual
Fear Factor.

**Living marked by the fear of God to transform a world cen-
tered on the fear of man requires personally trusting that salvation comes only by God's grace, and that subsequently you
do good deeds for His glory.**

Lesson #5: Don't be Afraid

> **Admiral McRaven:** "The pain of the 'Circuses'
> |two hours of extra calisthenics at the end of the
> day for those who failed to meet the required stan-
> dards for the day's physical training| built inner
> strength and physical resiliency. Life is filled
> with 'circuses.' You will fail. You will likely fail
> often. It will be painful. It will be discouraging.
> At times, it will test you to your very core. But, if
> you want to change the world, don't be afraid of
> the 'circuses.'"

Jesus knows His time has come. In mere hours, He will be
arrested, beaten to near-death, be forsaken by His heavenly Father,
and give up His Spirit. Jesus loves us so much that He willingly
endures the righteous wrath of a just God to pay the penalty for

our sin. But, Jesus also knows that He will overcome the world and its ruler. Because of this, Jesus looks to the future and focuses on His disciples, telling them—and also us who have placed our faith in Him—to have peace despite the many earthly trials and sorrows we have and will experience.[2] In other words, because of Jesus, don't be afraid of this world's "circuses." Have a healthy fear of God instead.

Living marked by the fear of God to transform a world centered on the fear of man requires finding peace in Jesus while enduring life's many trials and sorrows.

Lesson #6: Slide Head First

Admiral McRaven: "At least twice a week, the trainees were required to run the obstacle course. . . . But the most challenging obstacle was the 'Slide for Life.' It had a three-level, 30-foot tower at one end and a one-level tower at the other. In between was a 200-foot-long rope. You had to climb the three-tiered tower and, once at the top, you grabbed the rope, swung underneath the rope, and pulled yourself hand-over-hand until you got to the other end. The record for the obstacle course had stood for years. . . . The record seemed unbeatable. Until one day, a student decided to go down the 'Slide for Life" head first. . . . He bravely mounted the top of the rope and thrust himself forward. It was a dangerous move, seemingly foolish and fraught with risk. Failure could mean injury and being dropped from the course. Without hesitation, the student slid down the rope perilously fast. Instead of several minutes, it only took him half that time. And, by the end of the

---

[2] Jesus says in John 16:33 (ESV): "I have said these things to you, that in me you may have peace. In the world you will have tribulation. But take heart; I have overcome the world."

course, he had broken the record. If you want to
change the world, sometimes you have to slide
down the obstacles head first."

Living as a follower of Jesus Christ is radical and dangerous.
You're literally at war with Satan on his home turf. Every day,
flaming arrows shoot toward you, trying to make you jump to the
right or the left, toward the fear of man and toward personal comfort and ease, rooted in pride—the fear of self. But, if your eyes
are fixed straight ahead on Jesus, you will recall His following
statement:

> Then he said to the crowd, "If any of you wants
> to be my follower, you must give up your own
> way, take up your cross daily, and follow me. [24]
> If you try to hang on to your life, you will lose it.
> But if you give up your life for my sake, you will
> save it. [25] And what do you benefit if you gain the
> whole world but are yourself lost or destroyed?
> [26] If anyone is ashamed of me and my message,
> the Son of Man will be ashamed of that person
> when he returns in his glory and in the glory of
> the Father and the holy angels." (Luke 9:23–26)

To "give up your own way, take up your cross daily, and follow
me" means continuing to traverse the bridge of repentance that
leads upward from the dark and wide path. Repentance draws us
back to God. Our stubbornness pulls us away. So, we have to first
turn to our cross and recognize it for what it is: An instrument used
to kill a person. We then pick up our cross through the power of the
Holy Spirit, who then transforms our lives to be more like Christ's
as we follow His example. Picking up our cross daily is the process
of sanctification, increasing our Spiritual Fear Factor. But, if we try
to hold onto and save our lives marked by the fear of man, we will
be ashamed of Jesus and His message, ultimately losing our lives
in the end. Conversely, those who live with a high Spiritual Fear

Factor know this truth: If we lose our lives to follow Jesus today, then Jesus will save our lives for eternity.

Living marked by the fear of God to transform a world centered on the fear of man requires record-setting boldness to trust God's direction, allowing Him to be at work in and through you to share Jesus, so others may live for eternity.

Lesson #7: Don't Back Down

> **Admiral McRaven:** "During the land-warfare stage of training, the students are flown out to San Clemente Island . . . The waters off San Clemente are a breeding ground for the great white sharks. To pass Seal training, there are a series of long swims that must be completed. One is the night swim. Before the swim, the instructors joyfully brief the students on all the species of sharks that inhabit the waters off San Clemente. . . . But you are also taught that if a shark begins to circle your position, stand your ground. Do not swim away. Do not act afraid. And, if the shark . . . darts toward you, then summons up all your strength and punch him in the snout, and he will turn and swim away. There are a lot of sharks in the world. . . . So if you want to change the world, don't back down from the sharks."

Every day, those in the military stand their ground in the face of physical danger to save others. One day over 2,000 years ago, Jesus courageously endured the world's most painful physical death to save you and me by paying the spiritual penalty for our sins. Accordingly, every day, followers of Jesus are commanded to stand their ground in the face of spiritual danger. To review, the Apostle Paul closes his letter to the early church in the city of Ephesus with these instructions regarding spiritual warfare:

A final word: Be strong in the Lord and in his mighty power. [11] Put on all of God's armor so that you will be able to stand firm against all strategies of the devil. [12] For we are not fighting against flesh-and-blood enemies, but against evil rulers and authorities of the unseen world, against mighty powers in this dark world, and against evil spirits in the heavenly places.

[13] Therefore, put on every piece of God's armor so you will be able to resist the enemy in the time of evil. Then after the battle you will still be standing firm. [14] Stand your ground, putting on the belt of truth and the body armor of God's righteousness. [15] For shoes, put on the peace that comes from the Good News so that you will be fully prepared. [16] In addition to all of these, hold up the shield of faith to stop the fiery arrows of the devil. [17] Put on salvation as your helmet, and take the sword of the Spirit, which is the word of God.

[18] Pray in the Spirit at all times and on every occasion. Stay alert and be persistent in your prayers for all believers everywhere. (Ephesians 6:10–18)

Our enemy is Satan and those under his dominion. Our protection comes from God to enable us, just like an aspiring Navy Seal, to stand firm in the face of danger. For those with a high Spiritual Fear Factor, having faith in the truth of the Good News—a holy, righteous God making the way for salvation through Jesus—provides a peace that surpasses all understanding in the midst of battle. It's this defensive protection that stops the Devil's attacks. Then, just like the aspiring Seals, we can go on the offensive against the enemy. Instead of punching with our hands, we pierce our enemy with God's Word, which proclaims our eternal victory in Jesus and our enemy's eternal death. Together, victory is ours in Jesus, God's Word made flesh. Until the final battle, it's our responsibility to lift up our brothers and sisters on the spiritual battlefield in prayer. Through Jesus, we fight together—with a high Spiritual Fear Factor.

Living marked by the fear of God to transform a world centered on the fear of man requires standing your ground in Jesus and helping others to do the same, while fighting in the spiritual war being waged by the Devil.

Lesson #8: Be Your Very Best

Admiral McRaven: "As Navy Seals, one of our jobs is to conduct underwater attacks against enemy shipping. We practice this technique extensively. . . . The 'shiptack' mission is where a pair of Seal divers is dropped off outside an enemy harbor and then swims well over two miles underwater using nothing but a depth gauge and a compass . . . During the entire swim, even well below the surface, there is some light that comes through. It is comforting to know that there is open water above you. But, as you approach the ship . . . to a pier, the light begins to fade. The steel structure . . . blocks the moonlight . . . the surrounding street lamps. . . . all ambient light. To be successful . . . you have to swim under the ship and find the keel, the centerline, and the deepest part of the ship. . . . But, the keel is also the darkest part of the ship, where you cannot see your hand in front of your face. Where the noise from the ship's machinery is deafening. And where it gets to be easily disoriented. And you can fail. Every Seal knows that under the keel, at that darkest moment of the mission, is the time when you need to be calm. When you must be calm. When you must be composed. When all your tactical skills, your physical power, and your inner strength must be brought to bear. If

211

you want to change the world, you must be your
very best in the darkest moments."

One of the most quoted Bible verses is a lyric King David
penned in Psalm 23:4 (ESV): "Even though I walk through the
valley of the shadow of death, I will fear no evil, for you are with
me; your rod and your staff, they comfort me." The phrase "valley
of the shadow of death" can also be translated the "darkest valley."
Through training, a Seal brings his best in the darkest moments of
battle. Through Jesus, a Christian brings God's best in the darkest
moments of spiritual battle. The more training, the stronger the
Seal. The more fear of God, the stronger the Christian. Both the
Seal and Christian are calm, composed, and at their very best in
the battle's darkest moments.

**Living marked by the fear of God to transform a world cen-
tered on the fear of man requires being calm, composed, and
at your very best, through steadfast faith in God's guidance
and protection.**

Lesson #9: Sing in the Mud

Admiral McRaven: "The ninth week of training
is referred to as 'Hell Week.' It is six days of no
sleep, constant physical and mental harassment,
and one special day at the 'Mud Flats.' The 'Mud
Flats' are . . . a swampy patch of terrain where the
mud will engulf you. It is on Wednesday of 'Hell
Week' that you paddle down to the 'Mud Flats'
and spend the next fifteen hours trying to survive
the freezing cold, the howling wind, and the incessant pressure to quit from the instructors. As the
sun began to set . . . my training class . . . was
ordered into the mud. The mud consumed each
man 'til there was nothing visible but our heads.
The instructors told us we could leave the mud if
only five men would quit . . . just five men and

we could get out of the oppressive cold. Looking around the 'Mud Flat,' it was apparent that some students were about to give up. There were still over eight hours 'til the sun came up—eight more hours of bone-chilling cold. The chattering teeth and shivering moans . . . were so loud it was hard to hear anything. And then, one voice began to echo in through the night. One voice raised in song. The song was terribly out of tune, but sung with great enthusiasm. One voice became two, and two become three, and before long, everyone in the class was singing. The instructors threatened us with more time in the mud if we kept up the singing, but the singing persisted. And somehow the mud seemed a little warmer, and the wind a little tamer, and the dawn not so far away. If I have learned anything in my time traveling the world, it is the power of hope. The power of one person—a Washington, a Lincoln, King, Mandela, and even a young girl from Pakistan, Malala—one person can change the world by giving people hope. So, if you want to change the world, start singing when you're up to your neck in mud."

Author of over half the New Testament, the Apostle Paul can easily be regarded as one who's changed and influenced the world for Jesus more than any other. He had been up to his neck in mud many times over. In addition to being "given a thorn in [his] flesh, a messenger from Satan to torment [him],"[3] Paul details his "Mud Flat" experiences:

> I have worked harder, been put in prison more often, been whipped times without number, and faced death again and again. [24] Five different times the Jewish leaders gave me thirty-nine lashes. [25]

---

[3]   2 Corinthians 12:7b

Three times I was beaten with rods. Once I was stoned. Three times I was shipwrecked. Once I spent a whole night and a day adrift at sea. [26] I have traveled on many long journeys. I have faced danger from rivers and from robbers. I have faced danger from my own people, the Jews, as well as from the Gentiles. I have faced danger in the cities, in the deserts, and on the seas. And I have faced danger from men who claim to be believers but are not. [27] I have worked hard and long, enduring many sleepless nights. I have been hungry and thirsty and have often gone without food. I have shivered in the cold, without enough clothing to keep me warm. (2 Corinthians 11:23b–27)

Caked with mud and literally left for dead.[4] Yet Paul's singing echoes for eternity because of his fear of God. He sees the eternal picture and calls on followers of Jesus to sing in the mud:

We can rejoice, too, when we run into problems and trials, for we know that they help us develop endurance. [4] And endurance develops strength of character, and character strengthens our confident hope of salvation. [5] And this hope will not lead to disappointment. For we know how dearly God loves us, because he has given us the Holy Spirit to fill our hearts with his love. (Romans 5:3–5)

He outlines why we sing and rejoice when we're up to our necks in life's mud. The mud of life helps us develop the endurance to withstand it. Such endurance strengthens our character, increasing our Spiritual Fear Factor, which increases our confidence in the hope of salvation God freely gives us because of His love for us.

---

[4] Acts 14:19 (ESV): But Jews came from Antioch and Iconium, and having persuaded the crowds, they stoned Paul and dragged him out of the city, supposing that he was dead.

Oh, what a joy it is to know that God delights in those who fear Him and put their hope in His unfailing love! That's worth singing when we're up to our necks in mud!

Living marked by the fear of God to transform a world centered on the fear of man requires continually rejoicing in Jesus Christ, while enduring trials to strengthen you and develop your character.

Lesson #10: Never Give Up

> **Admiral McRaven:** "Finally, in Seal training there is a . . . brass bell that hangs in the center of the compound for all the students to see. All you have to do to quit is ring the bell. Ring the bell and you no longer have to wake up at five o'clock. Ring the bell and you no longer have to be in the freezing cold swims. Ring the bell and you no longer have to do the runs, the obstacle course, the PT, and you no longer have to endure the hardships of training. All you have to do is ring the bell to get out. If you want to change the world, don't ever, ever ring the bell."

In God's love for humanity, He never rings the bell. Because He first loved us, why would we ever consider ringing the bell? Why would we settle for a low Spiritual Fear Factor? The Apostle Paul writes:

> I don't mean to say that I have already . . . reached perfection. But I press on to possess that perfection for which Christ Jesus first possessed me. [13] No, dear brothers and sisters, I have not achieved it, but I focus on this one thing: Forgetting the past and looking forward to what lies ahead, [14] I press on to reach the end of the race and receive

the heavenly prize for which God, through Christ Jesus, is calling us. (Philippians 3:12–14)

You and I, as followers of Jesus, are called to press on and not to be held back by our past. That's to keep going, to keep looking forward, to embrace grace, to finish the race of life fearing God, and to ultimately receive a heavenly prize beyond our wildest dreams. We can run the world's race because of God's grace.

Living marked by the fear of God to transform a world centered on the fear of man requires a dogged determination to grow in the fear of God, until we experience Heaven's perfect love for all eternity.

Your Final James 1:22 Challenge

Congratulations, graduate! Your charge—until your heavenly graduation and glorification—is to live marked by fearing God. Or, as King Solomon writes in Ecclesiastes 12:13, "That's the whole story. Here now is my final conclusion: Fear God and obey his commands, for this is everyone's duty."

See who you are.
See who God is.
Believe what He has done, is doing, and will do.
Respond in obedience to Him.

And then watch God work in and through you to transform a world centered on the fear of man—all for God's glory!

Bibliography

Commencement:
The Beginning Introduction

1. http://www.cnn.com/2013/09/27/tech/social-media/apparently-this-matters-haunted-house/

2. http://www.statisticbrain.com/fear-phobia-statistics/

3. http://www.washingtonpost.com/wp-srv/nation/specials/attacked/transcripts/bushaddress_092001.html

Chapter 1:
History 101: The World's First Terrorist Attack

1. https://books.google.com/ngrams/graph?year_start=1800&-year_end=2008&corpus=15&smoothing=7&case_insen-sitive=on&content=terrorism&direct_url=t4%3B%2C-terrorism%3B%2Cc0%3B%2Cs0%3B%3Bterror-ism%3B%2Cc0%3B%3BTerrorism%3B%2Cc0%3B%3B-TERRORISM%3B%2Cc0

2. Definition based on http://www.britannica.com/topic/terrorism

Chapter 3:
Language 101: What Does It Mean to Biblically Fear God?

1. http://christianchat.com/bible-discussion-forum/28359-im-christian-but-i-am-afraid-god.html

2. http://www.hebrew4christians.com/Scripture/Parashah/
    Summaries/Eikev/Yirah/yirah.html

Chapter 4:
Language 102: What Does It Mean to Live in a Fear-Full World?

1. http://www.metrolyrics.com/the-fear-lyrics-lily-allen.html

2. http://www.usnews.com/news/articles/2012/04/24/
    fear-of-commitment-economy-drive-generation-y-shop-
    ping-patterns

3. http://www.cbsnews.com/news/
    what-is-causing-the-boomerang-generation/

4. http://www.usnews.com/news/articles/2014/11/13/
    average-student-loan-debt-hits-30–000

5. http://www.nytimes.com/2014/03/08/opinion/blow-the-self-
    ie-generation.html?_r=0

6. http://www.mediapost.com/publications/article/238983/mil-
    lennials-have-become-generation-fear.html

7. Martin, J. A. (1985). Luke. In J. F. Walvoord & R. B. Zuck
    (Eds.), *The Bible Knowledge Commentary: An Exposition
    of the Scriptures* (Vol. 2, pp. 226–227). Wheaton, IL:
    Victor Books.

8. Grassmick, J. D. (1985). Mark. In J. F. Walvoord & R.
    B. Zuck (Eds.), *The Bible Knowledge Commentary: An
    Exposition of the Scriptures* (Vol. 2, pp. 122–124). Wheaton,
    IL: Victor Books.

9. http://www.goodreads.com/quotes/tag/karma

10. Welch, Edward T. (1997). *When People Are Big and God Is Small*. (pp. 96–97). Phillipsburg, NJ: Presbyterian and Reformed Publishing Company.

Chapter 5:
Biology 101: Dissecting Spiritual Grasshoppers

1. http://alwayswellwithin.
   com/2011/11/03/37-inspiring-quotes-from-albert-einstein/

2. http://www.nato.int/nrdc-it/about/message_to_garcia.pdf

3. http://www.cs.cmu.edu/~moore/a_message_to_garcia.html

Chapter 6:
Math 101: Calculating Your Spiritual Fear Factor

1. https://www.washingtonpost.com/blogs/answer-sheet/
   post/no-algebra-isnt-necessary—and-yes-stem-is-over-
   rated/2012/08/26/edc47552-ed2d-11e1-b09d-07d971dee30a_
   blog.html

2. https://www.cs.cornell.edu/~kvikram/htmls/read/maths.htm

3. Rice, John R. (1943). *The Backslider* (pp. 4–5). Murfeesboro, TN: Sword of the Lord Publishers.

Chapter 7: Musing on Music

1. http://www.gizmag.com/
   western-music-universal-language/11246/

2. http://pharrellwilliams.com/

3. http://www.theblaze.com/stories/2014/09/17/which-famed-singer-just-said-its-incredibly-arrogant-and-pompous-to-reject-gods-existence/

4. https://play.google.com/music/preview/Tj7ujtq7hqfqv04fwuppfj7wt5y?lyrics=1&utm_source=google&utm_medium=search&utm_campaign=lyrics&p-campaignid=kp-lyrics

5. http://www.mtv.com/news/1591609/colbie-caillat-from-american-idol-reject-to-john-mayer-tourmate/

6. http://www.theatlantic.com/politics/archive/2014/01/spiritual-but-not-religious-a-rising-misunderstood-voting-bloc/283000/

7. http://hollowverse.com/colbie-caillat/

8. http://www.colbiecaillat.com/bio/

9. https://play.google.com/music/preview/Tkur2cfewqwlkofixx3bgqorvjq?lyrics=1&utm_source=google&utm_medium=search&utm_campaign=lyrics&p-campaignid=kp-songlyrics

Chapter 8: Knowing the Names

1. http://www.bartleby.com/70/3822.html

2. http://www.dailymail.co.uk/sciencetech/article-3083204/Why-never-remember-people-s-names-Brain-struggles-retain-random-information-especially-not-interested-person.html

3. https://www.blueletterbible.org/study/misc/name_god.cfm

4. http://www.biblestudy.org/beginner/different-names-for-jesus-in-bible.html

5. http://blogs.thegospelcoalition.org/justintaylor/2009/04/09/well-i-wonder-if-you-know-him/

6. http://articles.latimes.com/2000/apr/08/local/me-17324

7. https://thatsmyking.wordpress.com/biography/

Chapter 9: Walking in the World

1. http://www.thecrimson.com/column/a-dash-of-insanity/article/2015/4/13/nothing-we-do-matters/

2. http://www.andyandrews.com/ms/the-butterfly-effect/

3. http://www.technologyreview.com/article/422809/when-the-butterfly-effect-took-flight/

4. http://www.merriam-webster.com/dictionary/determinism

5. http://www.cbsnews.com/news/proving-the-butterfly-effect-with-a-single-act-of-kindness/

6. http://www.cnn.com/2012/12/04/business/digital-native-prensky/

7. Guinness, Oz. (2003). *The Call: Finding and Fulfilling the Purpose of Your Life*. (pp. 66–67). Nelson, Thomas, Inc.

8. http://www.theatlantic.com/business/archive/2015/05/why-emoji-are-suddenly-acceptable-at-work/393191/

9. http://emojipedia.org/face-screaming-in-fear/

Chapter 10: Surrendering Your Stone

1. http://www.brainyquote.com/quotes/quotes/i/iyanla-vanz519999.html?src=t_holding_on

2. http://www.brainyquote.com/quotes/quotes/b/bil-lygraha626354.html?src=t_character

3. http://www.nyc-architecture.com/GON/GON005.htm

4. http://www.oxfordlearnersdictionaries.com/us/definition/american_english/pregnant

Chapter 11: Freed Forever from Fear

1. http://www.brainyquote.com/quotes/quotes/l/luciu-sanna104795.html?src=t_eternity

2. http://gizmodo.com/a-brief-history-of-easter-eggs-in-tech-5900026

Commencement:
The Graduating Conclusion

1. https://www.youtube.com/watch?v=pxBQLF-Lei70&list=PLYDUT30CAaLvKDJXJV42cv-JeUqpNJLhWE

2. http://www.pewresearch.org fact-tank/2015/12/22/15-striking-findings-from-2015/

About the Author

T im Abraham is a Church Strategy and Leadership Consultant for The Malphurs Group, and Co-Founder and Member of Beyond Leading, a leadership and business consulting firm. He's served at the highest levels of state government and as a member of the executive leadership team for one of the largest churches in West Virginia.

Tim earned an MBA and multiple bachelor's degrees from West Virginia University and is a member of Phi Beta Kappa and Beta Gamma Sigma. He's attended executive education programs through Harvard University and the University of Pennsylvania. The Council of State Governments named Tim a Toll Fellow, after he participated in the nation's premier leadership development programs for state government offi-
cials. Among other honors received, the Commonwealth of Kentucky named him a Kentucky Colonel in recognition of his noteworthy accomplishments and outstanding service to the nation.

West Virginia Mountaineers at heart, Tim and his wife, Kelly, currently enjoy God's beautiful creation residing in Myrtle Beach, South Carolina.